To Lois and Bob
with all my
best wishes

Entertaining in the

NORTHWEST
Style

A MENU COOKBOOK

GREG ATKINSON

PHOTOGRAPHS *by* ANNE HERMAN

Greg Atkinson

November 2005

SASQUATCH BOOKS
SEATTLE

Copyright ©2005 by Greg Atkinson
All rights reserved. No portion of this book may be reproduced or utilized in any form, or by any
electronic, mechanical, or other means without the prior written permission of the publisher.

Printed in China
Published by Sasquatch Books
Distributed by Publishers Group West
10 09 08 07 06 05   8 7 6 5 4 3 2 1

Book design: Stewart A. Williams
Cover illustration: Molly Norris Curtis
Interior photographs: Anne Herman

ISBN 1-57061-436-9

Library of Congress Cataloging-in-Publication Data is available.

Sasquatch Books
119 South Main Street, Suite 400
Seattle, WA 98104
(206) 467-4300
www.sasquatchbooks.com
custserv@sasquatchbooks.com

CONTENTS

Acknowledgments

This book is dedicated to my parents, Tex and Annie. Learning to cook, I trashed their kitchen more times than I can count. But more than splattered walls and flour-covered floors, in the process of learning to be a fully realized human being, I created emotional messes that were far worse than the ones I left in their kitchen. Now, with two children of my own, I marvel at how they raised six of us born in a short seven years. And I recall with wonder the thousands of meals we took together around the round wooden table they bought when we moved into the house where they still live.

Now when I stand at the stove, I sense my mother's presence, encouraging me to pay attention to the food, to leave it alone when it needs to be left alone, and to watch for signs that it needs my attention. And whenever I sit down to write, I imagine how my father will respond when he reads it. I think his passion for the written word, deferred as it was so that he could provide for his family, is what motivated me to write. Wherever I have gone, whatever I have done, my parents have encouraged me to go there and do it, to be myself. And no matter how I rebelled against them or challenged their beliefs, they met me halfway and embraced me, their youngest son. Put simply, they have loved me, and for that I love them.

Perhaps because Tex and Annie used to tell me that I could do whatever I set my mind to, I once believed that I could write the book I had in my head. Now, as I send this, my fourth cookbook, to press, I have come to realize that a book has a life of its own. And bringing it into the world has shaped my writing and my cooking almost as much as I have shaped the book. Originally conceived as a collection of recipes that would represent the meals I was cooking as executive chef at Canlis restaurant in Seattle, the book, as it unfolded, became more and more about cooking and entertaining at home and in the homes of my friends. Those friends include my former bosses Chris and Alice Canlis, the owners of Canlis restaurant, who provided me with the most amazing opportunities for professional growth a chef could ever wish for, and to whom I am eternally grateful.

Long before the book was complete, even before I was finished at Canlis, I left the restaurant to launch the food and beverage programs at IslandWood, an outdoor education facility that sprang up in the woods near my home on Bainbridge Island. I am immensely grateful to Paul and Debbi Brainerd, the founders of IslandWood, for preserving that land and providing thousands of children with a window—both cognitive and corporal—into the natural world, a world from which we are all too often completely removed. And I thank Paul and Debbi for opening their home to me to prepare what I hope have been memorable meals that helped provide funding for the kids' programs at IslandWood.

My staff at IslandWood, especially Tom Loverich and Kerrie Sanson, made it possible for anything I could imagine to become real in that dining hall. With their help, I prepared some of the best meals I have ever cooked. I am also grateful to the school-age kids with whom I had the privilege to spend time there. They helped me realize how important food is to people in their formative years, how it shapes their understanding of the world, and how the food choices we make impact the natural systems of which we all are a part.

The kids shared family-style meals around tables in the dining hall, recycled their leftovers into compost that was eventually piled onto a display garden, and helped harvest some of the vegetables and herbs for their meals. Over the year and a half that I served as chef at IslandWood, the concept for this book continued to take shape, unfurling and refolding in on itself again and again like the leaves on a tree.

Most of the menus and recipes were at one time or another incorporated into a series of cooking classes that I taught at various cooking schools around Puget Sound. I am grateful to the directors of those schools for providing me with the opportunity to teach. And I am even more grateful to the students who asked tough questions, forcing me to view each recipe as if I had never prepared the dish before. This allowed me to correct many simple errors and to answer myriad questions that readers might have asked. I know the process made this a better book.

The recipes and menus were developed further when they were prepared in order to be photographed. When it came time to photograph the menus, I called on friends and asked if I could prepare the menus in their homes. Seeing my food re-created in others' kitchens and presented on their dishes at their tables allowed me to see how the dishes might be adapted to other people's equipment and incorporated into other people's lives. And I am very grateful to the hosts who invited me in with the photographer and her equipment to bring these menus to life. Thanks are due to Anne and Langdon Simons, Chris and Alice Canlis, Peter and Melissa Evans, Paul and Debbi Brainerd, Bruce and Nancy Williams, Michael and Marielle Macville, and Jerilyn Brusseau. And huge thanks to Anne Herman, who allowed all of us to act as on-the-spot food stylists, commentators, and photographic assistants.

To send this book out into the world in a fixed state, a printed form that may no longer be altered, seems odd to me. These essays, recipes, and menus have continually evolved over the years that it has taken me to compile them. But I suppose, as readers and cooks open the book to read the stories, to plan parties, or to use the recipes as a guide in the kitchen, these parts might continue to change, at least in the way they are perceived. So I am grateful to the people who will use it, keeping alive the flavors and feelings that motivated me to write it.

I thank Gary Luke, my patient and visionary editor, who has seen better than I have what each of my book proposals has held, and who has helped me steer my work toward a brighter manifestation of what it should be.

My hope is that readers and cooks will take from this book not only recipes and menu plans but frames of mind, humor, and delight, and perhaps a little of the sorrow and fear that went into it. This way, meals that arise from these pages will be seasoned not only with the salt and pepper and herbs listed among the ingredients but with that intangible, unnameable stuff that life is made of.

Finally, I would like to thank my wife, Betsy, who once, long ago, encouraged me to submit my first food stories to a small-town newspaper editor. After years of saying I would like to write about food, and after actually writing a series of sample articles, I got cold feet, and my fear of rejection nearly paralyzed me. "They're no good," I said. "The *Journal* doesn't want these! I'm no writer!" She placed a hand on each of my shoulders and gently forced me to look her in the eyes. When our eyes finally met, she smiled, and I smiled in spite of myself, and my great dramatic performance went to pieces.

"You are a writer," she began. "You have known you were a writer since you were eight years old. You told me so." She was beautiful, angry, and sincere. I was humbled. "You are also a great chef," she said, and hushed me when I scoffed. "No one is better qualified than you are to write about the food you love." There are moments when I believe she was right. Thank you, Betsy.

After *the* Egg Hunt
A Feast *for* Spring

DEVILED EGGS

BELGIAN ENDIVE *and* GRAPEFRUIT SALAD
   with GOAT CHEESE FRITTERS

GRILLED LEG *of* LAMB

POTATO *and* GARLIC FLANS

BROILED GREEN ASPARAGUS

CELIA'S CAKES

When Betty MacDonald wrote *The Egg & I,* which rocketed to the top of the bestseller lists in 1945 and inspired the classic movie starring Fred MacMurray and Claudette Colbert, she lived not far from where I live now. Her first place was in the Chimacum Valley, between Bainbridge Island and Port Townsend on the Olympic Peninsula; I drive by it now and then. Her second place was on Vashon Island, just south of Bainbridge.

Although the nation's perception of Washingtonians has broadened somewhat beyond the Ma and Pa Kettle types portrayed in MacDonald's stories, I would argue that, beneath our twenty-first-century airs, we are still a bunch of chicken-raising country hicks at heart. My neighbor, for example, works as a fashion model. She flies off every other week to be photographed wearing designer jeans and tank tops for the pages of various magazines and catalogs. At home, she is more likely to be found in cutoff shorts, pulling eggs out from under a chicken or spreading its manure around her perennial flower beds.

An egg, to paraphrase Gertrude Stein, is an egg is an egg. So why do we go to the trouble of raising our own chickens? It turns out that a really fresh egg from a happy chicken is another thing entirely. Most eggs come from factory farms, products more of industry than of nature. They tumble off an assembly line into cartons and are shipped hither and yon until we plunk them into our shopping carts and bring 'em on home.

But for those of us lucky enough to have tasted eggs raised right in our own backyards, factory-farmed eggs just won't do. I was still a college student in Bellingham when I got hooked on homegrown eggs. I went to school by day and worked in a restaurant by night. One of my neighbors kept a henhouse, and since her place was on my route, I started saving lettuce scraps from the restaurant to bring to her chickens in exchange for some of their eggs. Typically, I would carry the lettuce in a bag on my head. (In those days, I didn't own a car. I walked almost everywhere I went, and I carried a lot of things around on my head: books, laundry, lettuce leaves.) Over time the chickens came to know me, and they allowed me to reach into their nests and gather their eggs, warm and brown on the outside, clear and golden on the inside.

Once, walking toward home after closing the restaurant fairly late at night, I was bringing lettuce to the chickens and singing a song in what I thought was a fine operatic tenor. A window opened and a head popped out. "Shut up down there!" Subdued, I snuck into my neighbor's garden and deposited the lettuce. The next morning I came back for eggs, and once I got them in the kitchen, I started working on a batch of home-made noodles and finished my song. Ah, those were the days.

Ever since then, I've carried the notion that eventually I will have chickens—and therefore eggs—of my own. The closest I've come to setting up my own coop came a few years back, when I caught an episode of Martha Stewart's program on TV. She was featuring her Aracuña hens, and I dutifully made a list of what she told me I would need in order to get started. On the list were items like this: one rooster, twelve hens, a warming light for the chicks, some number of yards of chicken wire, and the building supplies for a sturdy henhouse. For a good thirty minutes, I was serious. Then I went off to work and forgot all about it.

The next day I saw the list without the rose-tinted hues of the television's cathode ray, and I came to my senses. Actually, it was Betsy who brought me to my senses. "What's this?" she wanted to know, holding the chicken shopping list accusingly between thumb and forefinger. I was like a kid with a candy wrapper under my bed; what could I say? My keeping chickens would probably not be a good idea; I can barely take care of my pet cockatiel.

Fortunately, a few of my neighbors are better equipped at this sort of thing than I am. In addition to the fashion model–cum–chicken farmer, I have a friend who lives not too far away whose daughter keeps chickens, and she is quick to provide me with eggs for a nominal fee that covers the cost of their feed. Another neighbor puts eggs for sale in a cooler by the driveway, and if I tuck a few dollars into a jar, I am allowed to take some away. Even when I don't get it together to make these simple arrangements, I can, if I am willing to pay a little extra, buy naturally raised, local eggs at the supermarket. Although I hardly ever eat eggs as a dish unto themselves, I use eggs in so many things I make that I can't imagine cooking without them.

As the late Julia Child once said, "Cooking without eggs isn't cooking at all." In a slim little volume of her thoughts about food and cooking called *Julia's Kitchen Wisdom,* she wrote, "Eggs appear throughout cookery not only as themselves—in their omelet, scrambled, poached, stuffed, and soft-boiled guises—but as puff producers in cakes and soufflés, as thickeners for sauces and custards, and, of course, as the starters for those two noble and addictive creations, Hollandaise and mayonnaise."

Eggs are a staple, right up there with flour, milk, and sugar. And just like those other icons of the American kitchen, they have been under attack in recent decades by well-meaning revolutionaries hoping to steer us all down a road to better nutrition through highly processed alternatives to simple foods, simply prepared. Once, though, eggs were simply nourishing and delicious, and we were all as innocent about any potential harm from eggs as I was when I walked down the street with lettuce on my head singing songs at midnight. And these days, with most of our food-related fear directed at high-carbohydrate foods, mad cows, and mercury-laden seafood, eggs are taking less heat.

In springtime, when that great festival of the egg known as Easter rolls around, I like to devil some eggs, dressing their yolks with that lovely egg-based sauce known as mayonnaise. I offer these up almost as if they were some kind of pagan sacrifice, and even people who are afraid of high cholesterol cannot seem to resist them. The feast progresses with other symbolic foods of spring: a picture-perfect salad, grilled leg of lamb served with an egg-bound custard of garlic and potatoes, asparagus spears in lemon-butter sauce, and Celia's Cakes, a particularly delectable family dessert made with egg-based sponge cakes. For me, though, the best part of the whole meal is that tray of humble deviled eggs resplendent on their bed of watercress.

The Day Before

The goat cheese fritters for the salad can be assembled a day or two in advance, and the grapefruit can be prepared ahead as well. This makes the fairly elaborate salad course appear incredibly easy on the day of the feast. Since the marinade is an essential element in the preparation of the lamb, it's almost mandatory that the leg of lamb be prepared largely in advance. Even the side dishes can be prepared ahead up to a point and finished just before serving. The cakes too should be set up ahead of time and finished with a dollop of whipped cream just before serving.

What to Pour

Grilled lamb cries out for wine made with the robust grapes associated with Rhône wines. Fortunately, those grapes are becoming increasingly popular with Washington grape producers. Syrah in particular has become something of a darling of the Washington wine industry. When it is paired with the grilled lamb in this menu, it is easy to see why.

On the Table

When I served this menu for a spring dinner at the home of a friend, she had dozens of small potted plants all over the house. The plants spoke eloquently and subtly of everything this time of year represents: rebirth, youth, and renewal.

Make It Simpler

It would be easy to make a meal of the deviled eggs alone, but you needn't be that spartan in order to make this meal more doable with less fuss. The goat cheese fritters could be eliminated in favor of a few crumbles of goat cheese tumbling over the salad. Potato flans are elegant, but simple mashed Yukon Gold potatoes would be fine, and if time is of the essence, skip the step of grilling the asparagus and serve it simply boiled in salted water. If the individual Celia's Cakes seem like more than you can handle, use the same elements to create a rectangular cake that can be served in slices.

DEVILED EGGS

Old-fashioned and easy-to-make deviled eggs are a welcome opener to a spring meal. With mustard and horseradish, this version provides a gentle, warm kick without the lingering heat of chile peppers.

MAKES 24

12 large Hard-Cooked Eggs (recipe follows)
1/3 cup Homemade Mayonnaise (recipe follows)
1 tablespoon Dijon mustard
1 tablespoon prepared horseradish
Kosher salt, to taste
1 bunch watercress or other greens

⊙ Peel the eggs, then slice them in half lengthwise and scoop the yolks into a small mixing bowl, keeping the whites intact. Set the whites aside.

⊙ Add the mayonnaise, mustard, horseradish, and salt to the yolks, mashing with a fork or stirring with a wire whisk until the ingredients are well combined. Transfer the yolk mixture to a self-sealing plastic food-storage bag, and snip off one end to make an impromptu pastry bag.

⊙ Arrange the watercress on a platter. Put the whites on top of the watercress and gently pipe the yolk mixture into the center of each egg white. Serve at once, or keep refrigerated until serving time.

Hard-Cooked Eggs

Between the raw egg in your refrigerator and the elusive goal of a perfectly hard-cooked egg lies a minefield of erroneous instructions. Every cookbook author seems to have a different formula. My rules of thumb are based on guidelines established by Molly Stevens, a contributing editor to Fine Cooking *magazine.*

⊙ In a saucepan, cover the eggs with tap water and bring to a gentle boil over medium-high heat. As soon as the water comes to a boil, reduce heat to low and set a timer for 8 minutes.

⊙ When the timer goes off, pour off the water and give the pan a vigorous shake to crack the eggs. Cover them with cold water, drain, and cover with cold water again. When the eggs are cold, peel them.

Homemade Mayonnaise

Homemade mayonnaise is far easier to make than most cooks know, and anyone who has grown accustomed to its clean, fresh taste will be hard-pressed to go back to the bottled variety. Serve it in salads or on sandwiches.

MAKES ABOUT 2½ CUPS

2 egg yolks

2 tablespoons white vinegar

1 tablespoon Dijon mustard

1 teaspoon kosher salt

¼ teaspoon ground white pepper

2 cups canola oil

⊙ In a food processor or a mixing bowl, whip egg yolks, vinegar, mustard, salt, and white pepper for about 1 minute, or until mixture is thoroughly combined.

⊙ With the food processor running or whisking continually, slowly stream in the canola oil, starting with just a few drops of oil at a time, then building to a slow but steady stream until all the oil is incorporated.

⊙ Transfer the mayonnaise to a jar and store, covered, in the refrigerator for up to 1 week.

BELGIAN ENDIVE *and* GRAPEFRUIT SALAD *with* GOAT CHEESE FRITTERS

With its stunning pink-on-white-on-green arrangement, this salad looks like a work of art, but it doesn't last long. With a perfect balance of bitter, salty, sour, and sweet, the flavor is so compelling that once the salad has been tasted, it disappears in a flash. Put it on the table before anyone sits down so everyone will have a moment to see it in its untouched glory.

SERVES 8

6 heads Belgian endive (enough to yield 40 nice leaves)
4 large red grapefruits
1 bunch watercress, or 2 cups packed spinach leaves
Goat Cheese Fritters (recipe follows)
Grapefruit Vinaigrette (recipe follows)
1 cup toasted walnuts

⊙ Trim the base from each head of Belgian endive. Pull the larger individual leaves from each head and set aside; discard the cores or save them for another use.

⊙ With a zester, remove the colorful outer rind from the grapefruit and reserve. (If no zester is available, remove the outer rind with a potato peeler and cut it with a paring knife into very thin strips.) With a sharp knife, cut the top and bottom from each grapefruit, then cut away the peel; remove any bits of white membrane left attached. Working over a mixing bowl to catch juice, remove each section by cutting along the membranes on either side. Cut in toward the center and then out. (Grapefruit may be prepared several hours in advance.) Reserve juice for vinaigrette.

⦿ Arrange 5 leaves of endive in a palm-leaf pattern on each serving plate. If using the spinach, roll the leaves lengthwise into a tight bundle and then cut them crosswise with a sharp knife into ⅛-inch ribbons. Place a section of grapefruit in each leaf and a bundle of watercress or spinach at the base of the endive leaves.

⦿ Just before serving, fry the goat cheese fritters as directed in the recipe and transfer them directly from hot oil to plates, resting the hot fritters on the bed of watercress. Drizzle each salad with about 2 tablespoons of the grapefruit vinaigrette and top with toasted walnuts. Serve at once.

Goat Cheese Fritters

A light and crispy coating of walnuts and bread crumbs surrounds soft, warm goat cheese, providing a dramatic contrast to the cold, bright flavors of the grapefruit salad. The match is seemingly made in heaven, but these fritters pair equally well with almost any salad greens. Try them later in the season with a salad of mixed greens and raspberries dressed in walnut oil and raspberry vinegar. They're also great served hot on top of soup.

MAKES 8

 I log (II ounces) soft white goat cheese
 ½ cup flour
 2 eggs
 2 tablespoons water
 I teaspoon kosher salt
 ½ cup bread crumbs or panko (Japanese bread crumbs)
 ½ cup walnuts, finely chopped
 Canola oil for frying

⊙ With a sharp knife dipped in hot water, cut cheese into 8 rounds, each about ¾ inch thick.

⊙ Line up three soup bowls. Put the flour in one bowl, beat the eggs with the water and salt in the second bowl, and put the bread crumbs and walnuts in the third bowl.

⊙ Roll each piece of cheese in flour, shaking off the excess. Dip each flour-coated round of cheese into the egg mixture, roll in bread crumbs to coat, and set aside. (The fritters may be prepared ahead up to this point and refrigerated for several hours or overnight.)

⊙ Just before serving, put enough canola oil in a frying pan to form a layer 1 inch deep. Heat the canola oil to 375°F, or until a 1-inch cube of bread floats immediately to the top and sizzles. Fry breaded cheese, two or three pieces at a time, for 2 minutes on each side, or until golden. Drain on paper towels.

Grapefruit Vinaigrette

Boiling the juice of the grapefruit concentrates its flavor and allows it to stand in for vinegar in an otherwise basic formula for vinaigrette. Here, walnut oil amplifies the nutty goodness of the walnut-crusted goat cheese fritters, but if walnut oil is unavailable, olive oil may be used.

MAKES ABOUT 1¼ CUPS

    1 cup fresh-squeezed grapefruit juice

    2 tablespoons sugar

    1 teaspoon kosher salt

    ½ teaspoon freshly ground black pepper

    1 cup walnut oil or olive oil

⊙ Boil the grapefruit juice with the sugar, salt, and pepper in a small nonreactive (stainless steel or enamel) saucepan until it is reduced to ⅓ cup. Take the pan off the heat and whisk in the walnut oil. Serve at once, or cover and keep refrigerated until serving time.

GRILLED LEG *of* LAMB

With the bone removed, a leg of lamb becomes a broad, thin sheet of meat that cooks uniformly on the grill, with lots of surface area exposed to the open flames. Before grilling, the meat is marinated in a mixture of olive oil and lemon; the marinade both tenderizes and flavors the meat.

SERVES 6

1 boneless leg of lamb, 2½ to 3 pounds

2 tablespoons kosher salt, or to taste

1 tablespoon freshly ground black pepper, or to taste

¼ cup fresh-squeezed lemon juice

½ cup olive oil

1 tablespoon dried oregano leaves

6 cloves garlic, finely chopped

⊙ If the leg of lamb comes rolled and bound up in string, unroll it. Season the meat generously with salt and pepper. Whisk together the lemon juice and the olive oil with the oregano and garlic. Roll the leg of lamb in the mixture to coat it. Allow the meat to marinate for several hours or overnight.

⊙ Preheat a gas or charcoal barbecue grill. If a larger grilling surface is available, heat one side extra hot and leave the other side cooler, to provide a hot area for searing the meat and a cooler area for slower cooking. Just before cooking, rub the cooking surface with olive oil.

⊙ Lift the meat out of the marinade and sear it for 2 minutes on the hot side of the grill; then move it to the cooler side of the grill and let it cook for about 8 minutes, basting it with any leftover marinade. Turn the meat, sear it for 2 minutes on the hot side, then move it to

13

the cooler side and let it cook until it is barely cooked through, about 8 minutes more. An instant-read thermometer inserted into the thickest part of the meat will register between 135°F (rare) and 150°F (medium). The meat will yield when pressed with a finger. When broiling the lamb in the oven, use the broiler at high heat to sear; then turn it off and close the oven door for slower cooking.

⊙ Take the lamb off the grill or remove it from the oven, and let it stand for 5 minutes before slicing. Slice it on a bias against the grain into ⅛-inch-thick slices. Arrange the slices on a platter or transfer at once to individual serving plates, and serve hot.

POTATO *and* GARLIC FLANS

Typically utilized in desserts, the technique for making a custard or flan can also be used to make delightfully savory dishes like this one. The same technique is employed in the Green Pea Flans (page 31), in the Spinach Flans (page 64), and in the Kabocha Squash Flans (page 140).

SERVES 6

2 medium-sized yellow-fleshed potatoes,
    such as Yukon Gold, about 1½ pounds
18 cloves garlic
1 cup heavy cream
1 teaspoon kosher salt
½ teaspoon ground white pepper
3 eggs

⊙ Preheat the oven to 375°F and butter six 4-ounce ramekins or glass custard cups. Place the cups in a baking dish that will comfortably hold them all.

⊙ Peel the potatoes and cut them into 1-inch dice. In a medium saucepan, cover the potatoes with water and boil over high heat until tender but not crumbling, about 15 minutes.

⊙ Meanwhile, in a separate small saucepan, cook the garlic with the cream over medium-high heat until the garlic is tender, about 15 minutes. When the potatoes are ready, drain them and put them in a large mixing bowl. Mash with a potato masher or wire whisk.

⊙ Put the cooked garlic and cream in a blender and purée until smooth. Add the salt, white pepper, and eggs to the garlic mixture, and pulse on and off until the mixture is smooth. Pour the garlic and cream mixture over the mashed potatoes and whisk until smooth. Distribute the potato mixture evenly between the custard cups.

⊙ Pour boiling water into the baking dish until it reaches halfway up the sides of the cups. Cover the baking dish with buttered baker's parchment and then with aluminum foil. Bake until the custards are set, about 20 minutes. Remove from oven and allow to stand for 10 minutes.

⊙ Serve the flans at once, or keep them warm in a 200°F oven for up to 1 hour, or refrigerate and then reheat as needed. To serve, loosen the edges of the flans with a spatula or knife, slipping the point of the spatula down the sides of the flans to let in enough air to release them. Invert onto plates and serve hot.

BROILED GREEN ASPARAGUS

Served for more than five decades at Seattle's venerable Canlis restaurant, lightly boiled asparagus grilled over an open flame eloquently speaks the language of spring. The hot grill vacated by a grilled leg of lamb provides an open invitation to prepare this easy and elegant side dish.

SERVES 6

2 pounds jumbo asparagus, about 30 spears
2 tablespoons olive oil
Kosher salt and freshly ground black pepper, to taste
Lemon-Butter Sauce (recipe follows)

⊙ Boil the asparagus in a large pot of salted water until it becomes a brighter green but remains crisp, about 2 minutes. Cool the boiled asparagus.

⊙ Take 5 spears of asparagus and turn them upside down so that all the tips are even. Trim about 2 inches from the base of the spears. Insert two bamboo skewers sideways through the row of spears to create a sort of mat of asparagus. Repeat this process with the remaining spears to make 6 "mats."

(The asparagus may be prepared ahead up to this point and kept refrigerated for several hours or overnight.)

⊙ Rub the asparagus mats with the olive oil and sprinkle with the salt and pepper.

⊙ Grill the asparagus mats over hot coals or under a very hot broiler until the surface of the spears is blistered, then turn the mats and grill the other side. Cook until the asparagus is heated through, about 2 minutes on each side. Drizzle with the lemon butter just before serving.

Lemon-Butter Sauce

A variation on the classic beurre blanc, that workhorse of French restaurant kitchens, lemon butter replaces white wine and shallots with a jolt of fresh-squeezed lemon juice. It comes together in minutes to brighten the taste of any green vegetable. It also makes a great weeknight sauce for chicken or broiled fish.

MAKES ABOUT 1/2 CUP
> **2 tablespoons fresh-squeezed lemon juice**
> **2 tablespoons heavy cream**
> **1/2 cup (1 stick) cold butter, cut into 1/2-inch bits**

◉ In a small saucepan over high heat, boil the lemon juice until it has almost completely evaporated. Add the cream and bring to a rapid boil. Whisk in the butter. When all the butter is emulsified into the liquid, remove the pan from the heat but keep warm until serving time.

CELIA'S CAKES

These charming individual serving–sized cakes were created in the 1920s by a homemaker in New Harmony, Indiana, who just happened to be my wife's paternal grandmother. Years ago, when I discovered her recipe, I started making them for the restaurant where I worked at the time. Overnight, they became the most popular item on the dessert menu.

MAKES I DOZEN 3-INCH CAKES
I Basic Sponge Cake (recipe follows)
2 cups heavy cream, chilled
1/4 cup confectioners' sugar
I teaspoon vanilla extract
Mocha Frosting (recipe follows)
2 cups shredded coconut, toasted and cooled
Strawberry Purée (recipe follows)

⊙ Prepare the sponge cake. When it is cool, use a 2½-inch biscuit cutter to cut it into 24 rounds.

⊙ Whip the chilled cream until it is stiff, then stir in the confectioners' sugar and vanilla extract. Put the sweetened whipped cream in a large self-sealing plastic food-storage bag, and snip off a corner to create an impromptu pastry bag.

⊙ Use about a third of the whipped cream to pipe a generous dollop onto 12 of the small cake rounds. Place the remaining 12 rounds on top of the cream to form 12 "sandwiches."

⊙ Spread the frosting around the sides of each cake, leaving the tops unfrosted. As each cake is frosted, roll it in the toasted coconut. Pipe the remaining whipped cream on top of each cake and serve.

Note: The cakes may be filled, frosted, and rolled in coconut, then wrapped individually in plastic wrap and refrigerated without the whipped cream on top. Just before serving, place the cakes on serving plates and apply the final topping of whipped cream.

Basic Sponge Cake

MAKES ONE 11- BY 17-INCH CAKE

9 eggs, separated into whites and yolks
1½ cups sugar, divided
½ teaspoon salt
¾ cup (1½ sticks) butter, melted and cooled
2 teaspoons vanilla extract
1½ cups flour

⊙ Preheat the oven to 350°F and butter an 11- by 17-inch jelly-roll pan.

⊙ In a large mixing bowl, combine the egg yolks with ¾ cup of the sugar. Beat with a wire whisk until smooth. Stir in the salt, butter, and vanilla extract.

⊙ In a separate large, dry mixing bowl, beat the egg whites until they hold soft peaks, then add the remaining sugar gradually, beating all the while.

⊙ Fold one-third of the egg whites and half of the flour into the yolk mixture, stirring just until lumps are gone. Fold in another third of the egg whites and the remainder of the flour. Fold in the remaining egg whites.

⊙ Transfer the batter to the jelly-roll pan and bake until the cake is golden brown and springs back when pressed lightly in the center, about 25 minutes. Transfer the cake to a cooling rack and allow to cool for 10 minutes. Turn it out of the pan and cool completely.

Mocha Frosting

3 cups confectioners' sugar, divided
1/4 cup cocoa powder
1/4 teaspoon salt
1/4 cup (1/2 stick) butter, melted
1/3 cup strong coffee
1 teaspoon vanilla extract

⊙ In a large mixing bowl, with a whisk combine 2 cups of the confectioners' sugar, the cocoa, and the salt. Stir in the melted butter. Add the coffee and vanilla extract, stirring until smooth. Stir in the remaining confectioners' sugar.

Strawberry Purée

MAKES ABOUT 1 1/2 CUPS
1 pint strawberries, trimmed
2 tablespoons sugar
1 tablespoon lemon juice

⊙ Put the strawberries in a blender with the sugar and lemon juice, and purée until smooth.

When *the* Salmon Come Home

Celebrating *the* First Spring Salmon

KUMAMOTO OYSTERS *with* FROZEN RHUBARB MIGNONETTE

GREEN PEA FLANS *with* SAUTÉED PEA VINES *and*
    MOREL MUSHROOMS

GRILLED ALASKA SALMON

ASPARAGUS *and* RED POTATOES *with* CHIVE OIL

RHUBARB *and* ORANGE TART

It was 5 a.m., and even though I didn't get to bed until almost midnight, I was wide awake. Bed was on a boat anchored near the mouth of Copper River near Cordova, Alaska. Diesel fumes found their way up from the engine room, and the silver glow of a sun barely dipping below the horizon filled the cabin with eerie light. What made it impossible to get back to sleep, though, was the knowledge that in less than two hours "the season" would begin, and in a matter of minutes the world's best salmon would be pulled from its home waters.

By 7:00, I was standing on the deck of a thirty-two-foot aluminum bow picker called the *Whatever . . .* , designed to fish the dangerous delta flats—notorious for storms, ocean swells, and shifting shallows—watching a man named Pip Fillingham lower a gill net into the water. On board with me were three other men as determined as I was to help perpetuate the enthusiasm that surrounds the arrival of this fish on the market every year. Eric Chappell from Pacific Seafood was our host. Seattle chef Dan Thiessen was ready to phone in a report to be aired live on the Fox network's Seattle affiliate KCPQ as soon as a fish came on board. And photographer Marc Lester from the *Anchorage Daily News,* moonlighting on a book project, was snapping pictures like crazy.

For a long time I have been singing the praises of Copper River salmon, and people often want to know, "Does it really merit all the hype?" I always pipe back a wholehearted *yes,* citing a well-rehearsed refrain of clean clear water, omega-3 fatty acids, and wild and wonderful fish whose well-being helps sustain a wild and wonderful world. But I have to say that until I was there, surrounded by the majesty and anticipation of opening day, I was ill equipped to explain exactly why it is that I love these fish so much.

It's true that salmon from this particular fishery have been showered with more ink and airtime than the average candidate for president, but Copper River salmon are truly remarkable and unique. Wherever they hail from, a king is a king and a sockeye is a sockeye. But just as cabernet grapes grown in Washington's Columbia Valley are different from cabernet grapes grown in California's Napa Valley, so the salmon population from a particular river is different than salmon from anywhere else.

Situated as it is at the wide, cold delta of this magnificent river that flows into the Gulf of Alaska near Prince William Sound, this fishery demands that its denizens be fortified with a great deal of energy in order to make the perilous journey to their spawning grounds. Between the ocean swells that break against the first sandbars along the sixty-mile stretch of delta and the first splash of pure river water, there lies an intricate patchwork of land and water, salty and fresh, covering 750,000 acres. To make the trip, salmon store energy in the form of fat, and a good deal of that fat is of the variety we call omega-3. It lowers cholesterol, protects our blood vessels from damage due to stress and overnourishment, and may reduce the risk of certain cancers.

Connoisseurs have long maintained that this fat is what makes wild salmon so delectable, and I count myself among them. But there is more to the enjoyment of these salmon than health benefits or sensory pleasure. Sure, there's the rush of the ocean in its aroma. And the appearance of the fish, whether on the plate or still glistening in the round, does recall the primordial stuff we're all made of. Even the feel of this fish in the mouth is an awakening of the sense of touch; properly cooked, its surface is faintly crisped, its interior smooth and voluptuous. But there is also a kind of psychic joy in knowing that this is one of the last good things on earth, food in a state of Eden—pure, unadulterated excellence. I admit that I am almost as enamored of the mystique that surrounds the gathering and marketing of this fish as I am of the fish itself.

Fiercely eccentric and wildly courageous, the four hundred souls who derive their livelihood by fishing for Copper River salmon have as tenuous a hold on their way of life as the fish they pursue. To say that this fishery is vital to the local economy would be a gross understatement. The copper mines are used up. Shores that once boasted the heartiest population of razor clams in North America were destroyed by the Good Friday earthquake in 1964, and they have never recovered. Herring that once accounted for 20 to 30 percent of the fleet's annual revenue disappeared in the wake of the *Exxon Valdez* disaster in 1989.

And in the last ten years, exponential growth in salmon farms in the Lower 48 has caused the price of most Alaska salmon to plummet.

I used to think that Copper River season was a bonus on top of a healthy economy; rather, it appears to be the last functional piece of a crumbling system. Without being there on opening day, I never would have known that on the day before the opening everyone in Cordova is pumped up, worried sick, and filled with hope as bright and rich as the red-toned flesh of a sockeye salmon. When we went to the store to buy some snacks (eight dollars for a bunch of grapes!), everyone I saw was smiling. I asked if everyone always smiles in Cordova. "They do on the night before opening day!" I was told.

Every time I overheard a conversation in the bar, on the street, in the store, or on the ship-to-shore radio, I was inexplicably moved by the passion in the voices of these people when they wished one another well. "Stay safe!" ends one message. "Be careful," finishes the next one. It's as if they were going to war; "Good luck," says another one. Every fisherman is genuinely concerned about the safety of the others and presumably about his own. Maybe I'm just sleep-deprived, but I find this incredibly moving.

In Seattle, dead fish in a box represent a lucrative commodity; here in Alaska, the living salmon are an elusive prey whose capture and death mean survival for the hunter. And if this fishery works in part because a lot of media hype keeps the price at a level that will provide the fishermen with a sustainable living, then I say long live the media hype. More important, if it takes a lot of hype to make us mindful of what we are eating, to wake us from our farm-raised, overfed, trans-fatty-acid-induced stupor, then I say on with the hype, sound the alarm, wake up and smell the Copper River salmon!

What to Pour

Oysters and champagne, anyone? Dry sparkling wine is good with oysters. So is any crisp white wine. The green pea flans, which serve as a soup/salad course in this menu, are surprisingly sweet, but the meaty taste of the morel mushrooms and the grassy green flavor of the pea vines make for some interesting wine choices. Anything from a clean, dry sauvignon blanc like the one you may have poured with the oysters to an oaky and buttery chardonnay will go well with the flan. Pinot noir from Oregon is the standard pairing with grilled salmon, and it works perfectly here. If you want a dessert wine, a late-harvest Gewürztraminer is one good choice; any good ice wine would also work. As an interesting alternative, it would be perfectly appropriate to serve one good red Burgundy with both courses, and then dispense with wine in favor of mint tea or coffee upon the arrival of the dessert.

On the Table

Since the first salmon comes in at the peak of the flower season, it's easy to fill a vase with pickings from the garden or a local farmers market. The first time I designed a menu around Copper River salmon for a special event at Canlis restaurant, I wanted to emphasize the stark, clean beauty of spring. So I asked Jinnie McCormick, who provided the flowers for the restaurant, to sprout some wheatgrass for the centerpieces at every table. She used shallow baskets of the grass, and we studded them with hard-cooked quail eggs. Since then I have discovered that many supermarkets carry already-sprouted wheatgrass in the produce section. It makes a good centerpiece for any spring meal.

The Day Before

The green pea flans can be made a day ahead. Either make the custard base the day before and bake the flans the day of the dinner, or bake the flans in advance, then chill and reheat them. The asparagus should not be prepared too far in advance or it may lose some of its appeal. But if it's purchased the day before, it can be cut to serving length and then stored, cut side down, in water as if it were a bouquet of fresh-cut flowers. Both the shell and the filling for the rhubarb tart can be made a day in advance, but the final assembly of the tart should take place no earlier than the afternoon of the dinner.

Make It Simpler

Frozen rhubarb mignonette is a novel but nonessential way to garnish an oyster. The oysters may be presented without any sauce at all or with squeezes of lemon. In a pinch the green pea flans may be replaced with a simple green salad.

KUMAMOTO OYSTERS *with* FROZEN RHUBARB MIGNONETTE

Rhubarb, the proverbial "pie plant," is closely related to garden sorrel, and its bright, tangy, vegetal flavor is mirrored in its juice. In this recipe, the zippy juice fills in for vinegar in a traditional mignonette that is served frozen. Because they are small and easy to eat in one bite, Kumamotos are preferred, but the sauce would be equally delectable on any small oysters on the half shell.

SERVES 6

3 dozen live Kumamoto oysters
1/2 cup fresh rhubarb juice (see note)
2 tablespoons finely chopped shallots
1 teaspoon coarsely ground black pepper

Note: Rhubarb juice can be made by putting fresh rhubarb through a vegetable juicer. If no juicer is available, chop the rhubarb into 1-inch pieces, purée it in the blender with 2 to 3 tablespoons of cold water, then strain out the solids.

◉ As soon as the oysters come into the kitchen, arrange them in a single layer in a baking dish, taking care to make sure they are right side up—that is, the bowl shape should be down and the flat "lid" should be up. Cover them with damp paper towels and put the pan in the refrigerator until just before serving time. Stored in this way, fresh, live oysters should stay that way for three days.

◉ To make the rhubarb mignonette, combine the juice, shallots, and pepper and pour into in a small ice cream maker such as a Donvier, then stir or crank until the mixture is uniformly soft-frozen, about 10 minutes. (If no ice cream maker is available, put the mixture in an ice cube tray and freeze, undisturbed, for half an hour; then stir to break up any

29

crystals and freeze again, stirring every 15 minutes until the mixture is smooth, about an hour altogether.) If stored in the freezer the mixture will become hard-frozen, but it may be partially thawed and stirred to make it soft-frozen once again.

⦿ Carefully shuck the oysters, one at a time: Place an oyster cupped side down on a stable work surface. Using a towel to protect your hand from the sharp edges of the shell, hold the oyster firmly in one hand while you insert an oyster knife with the other. Push the knife in a short way and slide it under the top shell to cut the abductor muscle that holds the shell shut. Remove the top shell, then slide the knife under the meat of the oyster to free it from the bottom shell.

⦿ Serve the shucked oysters, 6 per serving, on a bed of ice with a spoonful of the mignonette on top of each one.

GREEN PEA FLANS *with* SAUTÉED PEA VINES *and* MOREL MUSHROOMS

I was introduced to vegetable flans by that old French master Roger Vergé, under whose tutelage I learned to make them. I use the same basic method to make potato flans, spinach flans, and kabocha squash flans in this book. The technique is especially useful in these menus because the flans can be made ahead and held at serving temperature, or chilled and reheated. I rely on disposable 4-ounce aluminum soufflé cups to bake my flans in individual-sized portions, but ceramic soufflé dishes or ramekins can also be used. (In a pinch you can use muffin cups, but since they are a little smaller than the 4-ounce dishes, this recipe will fill nine muffin cups, and turning the flans out of the muffin cups is tricky.)

SERVES 6

$1/4$ cup ($1/2$ stick) butter

I cup thinly sliced yellow onion

2 cups shelled green peas, or I package (10 ounces) frozen

$1/2$ cup heavy cream

4 eggs

I teaspoon salt

Sautéed Pea Vines and Morel Mushrooms (recipe follows)

⊙ Preheat the oven to 400°F and butter six disposable 4-ounce aluminum soufflé cups. Arrange the cups in a baking dish that will comfortably hold them all.

⊙ In a large skillet or saucepan, melt the butter over medium heat and cook the onion, stirring often, until tender but not brown, about 5 minutes.

31

⊙ Add peas and cream, bring the mixture to a boil, cover, and reduce heat to low. Simmer gently just until the peas are heated through, about 5 minutes.

⊙ In a blender or food processor, combine eggs with salt. Pulse on and off until smooth, then add the cooked pea mixture. Secure the lid and drape a kitchen towel over the top of the blender to prevent splashing. Pulse the pea mixture until smooth, using short pulses at first so that the hot mixture does not overflow. Distribute the purée evenly between the soufflé cups.

⊙ Pour boiling water into the baking dish until it reaches halfway up the sides of the cups. Cover the baking dish with buttered baker's parchment and then with aluminum foil. Bake for 25 to 30 minutes, or until a knife inserted in the center comes out clean.

⊙ Serve the flans at once, or keep them warm in a 200°F oven for up to 1 hour, or refrigerate and then reheat as needed. To serve, loosen the edges of the flans with a spatula or knife, slipping the point of the spatula down the sides of the flans to let in enough air to release them. Invert onto plates and serve hot with the pea vines and morels.

Sautéed Pea Vines *and* Morel Mushrooms

Years ago, after I first encountered pea vines in Vancouver's Chinatown, I discovered that adding a few of them to any dish of peas provides an extra green kick. Fresh morel mushrooms are available only in the spring; dried morels may be substituted for fresh, but they should be soaked for 10 minutes in boiling water before cooking. The liquid in which the dried morels were soaked should be used in the sauce; if you use dried morels in this recipe, the soaking liquid can be used in place of the chicken broth.

SERVES 6

1 pound tender young pea vines, or tender spring greens

1/2 cup chicken broth or morel-soaking liquid

2 tablespoons Chinese oyster sauce

1 teaspoon cornstarch

4 tablespoons olive oil, divided

Kosher salt and freshly ground black pepper, to taste

1/2 pound small fresh morels

⊙ Rinse the pea vines and shake off the excess water. In a small mixing bowl, stir together the chicken broth, oyster sauce, and cornstarch and place near the stove so the liquid will be ready to add when the time comes.

⊙ Heat a large sauté pan or a wok over medium-high heat. Put 2 tablespoons of the olive oil in the pan and sprinkle on generous pinches of salt and pepper. Toss in the morels and sauté until they are heated through, about 2 minutes.

⊙ Add the pea vines and the remaining olive oil. Move the greens quickly around the pan with tongs just long enough to distribute the oil evenly over the surface of the vegetable, about 1 minute.

⊙ Add the chicken broth mixture all at once to the hot pan. Toss for 1 minute, or until the liquid is reduced to a shiny glaze, and serve with green pea flans.

GRILLED ALASKA SALMON

I usually serve grilled salmon with some kind of sauce, but when the great runs like Copper River and Yukon River are in full swing and wild salmon is at its peak, the fish stands on its own, simply grilled and otherwise unadulterated. In this menu the salmon is served on a bed of flavorful spring asparagus and potatoes tossed with chive oil. This vegetable accompaniment serves the function of sauce, enhancing the salmon without detracting from it.

SERVES 6

Six salmon fillets (1½ inches thick), about 8 ounces each

3 tablespoons canola oil

Sea salt, to taste

◉ Build a fire in your backyard barbecue using your choice of charcoal or hardwood, or a combination. Allow the fire to blaze and then settle into a pile of coals. A bed of embers spotted with small, lively flames is the goal. Wipe a rack with an oily cloth and position it about 6 inches above the coals. (Alternatively, heat a stove-top grill over high heat until a few drops of water bounce and evaporate immediately on its surface.)

◉ Coat the salmon fillets lightly with the canola oil and sprinkle with the sea salt. Place the fillets, skin side up, on the grill and broil until the fish has nice chocolate-brown stripes from the grill, about 5 minutes. (If the oil ignites while the salmon is grilling, cool the flames with a little water, either splashing it on or using a squirt gun; otherwise, smoke from the flames will leave an oily black residue on the fish.) With a long spatula, turn the fillets once and broil until the sides show spots of white that look like cooked egg whites, about 3 minutes more.

⊙ Lift the salmon fillets off the grill and put them on a flat baking sheet, skin side down. If the salmon needs to cook a little longer, pop it into a preheated 350°F oven for a couple of minutes.

⊙ When the salmon is done, gently shimmy a spatula between the fish and the skin, leaving the skin behind on the baking sheet. Move the grilled and skinned salmon portions to a platter lined with the asparagus and potatoes, and serve at once.

ASPARAGUS *and* RED POTATOES *with* CHIVE OIL

Asparagus is the quintessential herald of spring. At the very beginning of the season asparagus is sometimes sold ungraded, and the bundles are composed of random spears of various sizes. I think they look wild and fun, most like the bundles I pick from my own garden, so if they are available, I opt for them. If a choice of thin or fat spears is offered, go for the fattest spears you can find; they have a higher ratio of insides to outsides, and the tender innards are the best part. Cooking the asparagus right in the pan with the potatoes makes this side dish super-simple. If two cooks are working together to prepare the meal, the dish can be prepared and served at once. Otherwise, the vegetables can be prepared ahead up to a point and finished just before serving.

SERVES 6

8 cups water

I tablespoon salt

3 pounds small red-skinned potatoes, cut in thirds

2 pounds jumbo asparagus, about 24 spears

²/₃ cup Chive Oil (recipe follows)

Chive blossoms or green onions, thinly sliced, for garnish

Additional salt and freshly ground black pepper, to taste

⊙ Put the water, salt, and potatoes in a heavy, 1-gallon stockpot over high heat and bring to a full, rolling boil. Reduce heat to low and cook until the potatoes are just barely fork-tender, about 10 minutes.

⊙ Meanwhile, cut the asparagus into 6-inch spears and drop it into the boiling water with the potatoes. Cook just until the asparagus is a darker green and is heated through, about 3 minutes. Drain the potatoes and asparagus and scatter them over a baking sheet to cool. (The vegetables may be prepared up to this point a couple of hours in advance and finished just before serving.)

⊙ Preheat the oven to 350°F. Five minutes before serving the vegetables, toss them with the chive oil in a large mixing bowl. Pop them in the oven just until they are heated through again, 3 to 5 minutes. Transfer the hot vegetables to a serving platter, sprinkle them with a shower of chive blossoms, and season to taste with additional salt and pepper. Serve at once.

Chive Oil

Late spring and early summer, the times of year when salmon is at its peak, are also the seasons when chives are blooming. If you don't grow your own, look for them at farmers' markets. The clusters of tiny lilies look like purple pompoms. Pulled off the cluster, the little flowers are flared trumpets announcing spring with a spray of fresh onion flavor. I like to serve spring vegetables tossed with oil that I've infused with chives—this takes only a moment in the blender—and then sprinkle the oiled vegetables with chive blossoms. Even if you cannot get the blossoms, the resulting flavor is wonderful. If chives or their blossoms are unavailable, the green part from green onions can be used in place of the chives, and the white part can stand in for the blossoms.

MAKES ABOUT ²/₃ CUP
> 1 bunch chives
> ²/₃ cup extra-virgin olive oil

◉ Put the chives and the oil in a blender and purée until smooth. Pass the purée through a wire-mesh strainer to remove the solids; a small amount of the volume may be lost in the process.

RHUBARB *and* ORANGE TART

Often paired with strawberries, rhubarb is coupled here with orange; the combination surprises and refreshes. If the punch of rhubarb's sourness needs a little mellowing, stir the optional butter into this filling. If a tangier filling is desired, or if the calorie count is a concern, leave it out. The filling and crust are made separately and assembled before serving.

SERVES 8
> 12 ounces (³/₄ pound) fresh rhubarb, sliced
> 1 cup sugar
> Grated zest and juice from 1 large orange
> ³/₈ cup (6 tablespoons) cornstarch
> ¹/₄ cup (¹/₂ stick) butter (optional)
> Butter Pastry (recipe follows)
> Violas for garnish

◉ Put the rhubarb and sugar in a large dry saucepan over high heat and cook, stirring, until the rhubarb releases some of its juices and the sugar is dissolved. Reduce heat to medium and simmer for 5 minutes, or until rhubarb is falling apart.

⊙ Put the orange zest and orange juice in a small mixing bowl with the cornstarch and whisk until smooth. Add a spoonful of the hot rhubarb and whisk again.

⊙ Add the orange mixture to the saucepan and cook 1 minute or until the sauce comes to a boil; it should be thickened and glossy.

⊙ Stir in the butter, if desired. Spread the filling in a shallow container and refrigerate until chilled and set.

⊙ Put the chilled filling in a self-sealing plastic food-storage bag, cut off one corner to make an impromptu pastry bag, and pipe the filling onto the baked and cooled butter pastry. Sprinkle viola petals over the tart and serve.

Butter Pastry

MAKES ENOUGH FOR ONE 6- BY 12-INCH TART
>   1 cup all-purpose flour
> $1/2$ cup (1 stick) cold unsalted butter, cut into $1/2$-inch bits
>   1 teaspoon salt
>   3 tablespoons cold water

⊙ Preheat the oven to 400°F and line a large baking sheet with baker's parchment.

⊙ In a food processor, combine the flour, butter, and salt. Process just until mixture resembles coarse crumbs. (If no food processor is available, combine the flour and salt in a large mixing bowl and cut in the butter with a pastry cutter, a fork, or your fingers.)

◉ Transfer the flour-and-butter mixture to a medium mixing bowl and sprinkle the cold water on top. Work the water into the flour mixture just until the dough comes together into a scrappy mass; do not knead or overwork.

◉ On a well-floured surface, roll the dough into a large rectangle, about 12 by 6 inches. Using a pizza cutter, trim the dough, then put it on the baking sheet.

◉ Score the dough with a fork to prevent it from puffing up too much in the oven. Bake for 15 to 18 minutes or until slightly puffed and golden brown. Cool the pastry before filling.

On Board *Carmelita*
Brunch *on the* Lake

|||||||||||||||||||||||||||||||||||||||||||||||||||||||||||||||||||||||||||||||||||||||||||||||||||||||||||||||||||||||||||||||||||||||||||||||||||||||||||||||||||

ORANGE *and* CURRANT SCONES

SAUSAGE STOLLEN *with* POACHED EGGS
    and LEMON HOLLANDAISE

YOGURT CREAMS *with* BALSAMIC STRAWBERRIES

When my friend Melissa Evans stocks the galley for a cruise on *Carmelita,* she has to plan carefully. Cruises on the sixty-five-foot motor yacht may extend for two weeks between provisioning stops, and the cruises often include twelve guests. But Melissa takes it in stride. A world traveler since childhood, she was born into a family of mariners known for their love of fine food. This sort of thing comes naturally to her, and other boaters could learn a lot from her casually professional command of the galley. I certainly have.

Several times over the years the Evanses and I have joined forces to auction off a brunch or a dinner on *Carmelita.* The proceeds go to charity. Now, after working beside Melissa in the galley on *Carmelita* a few times, I have come to view any cooking job outside my own home or a restaurant as a kind of cruise. As much as possible, I follow Melissa's example and do the majority of the cooking in advance. Then, when it comes time to cook and serve the meal, it's really just a matter of finishing things off. This approach is especially helpful if I'm actually planning to join in the meal.

"Even for those long cruises," says Melissa, "almost all the work is done before we set out." Weeks before a trip, she writes the menus and translates the recipes into shopping lists. "Once we're under way, the rest is easy." Careful planning is the key. "For the first few days I can use fresh milk and vegetables," but later in the trip, "I start to rely on powdered milk, and canned or frozen vegetables."

Melissa and her husband, Peter, have been cruising side by side for more than a decade. Even before *Carmelita,* Peter skippered numerous on-board seminars and workshops while navigating the inland waterway between Seattle and Juneau, Alaska. All the while, Melissa, a mother of two, worked beside him, manning the galley and sharing his love of the boating life. Commissioned by Melissa's uncle, Norton, in 1935, *Carmelita* seems made for the Evanses. They bought the boat from his estate in 1995 and refurbished it without compromising its classic style. In addition to lots of new paint and upholstery, the boat received new wiring throughout and a commercial-quality Five Star–brand range, so the galley is state of the art.

On board Melissa bakes fresh bread, and even though she doesn't use a bread machine, she buys bread machine mixes because everything is premeasured. "The bags always have instructions for doing it manually, and I just follow those." Other breads are started at home and finished on board. "I want to serve something homemade at breakfast, but I don't want to get up at six o'clock in the morning." Batter for muffins is assembled the night before and stays in the galley refrigerator until the strategic hour, when the scent of these irresistible baked goods comes wafting into every passenger's cabin on a sea breeze.

Melissa's keen sense of timing is matched by her style. Like chefs on the large cruise ships, she understands that food on board is more than sustenance, it's entertainment. Simple dishes are made extraordinary by creative presentations. Hot cereal, for instance, is served with maple leaf candies for garnish, and several days into the voyage, colorful slices of honeydew melon appear as if by magic. Unlike berries, she says, "Melons keep for days. I can pull out a honeydew or a cantaloupe four or five days into the trip and it's wonderful." A few thin slices are welcome fresh additions to the breakfast plates. "I can get a lot of mileage out of a good melon."

There are limitations to cooking at sea, but there are advantages too. Obviously, one can't shop for fresh food every day, but on the boat there is more time to cook. "On the boat, I actually do more cooking from scratch than I do at home. It may sound trite, but when we're under way and I'm in the galley, cutting vegetables or slicing melons, there's a kind of Zen. There's no stress. I'm putting together a meal I planned weeks in advance, and the phone doesn't ring, and I have a wonderful sense of being only where I am and doing only what I am doing at that moment."

I hope anyone preparing this menu for friends will feel the same way. I have prepared this brunch several times on board *Carmelita* and in other settings, with slight variations, and since most of the work is done in advance, cooking and serving it is a snap. Even when I am not serving this menu on a boat, I do as much as possible in advance, so that I can spend the morning casually applying the finishing touches and enjoying the company of my brunch guests.

The Day Before

Mix dry ingredients for the scones and put them in a self-sealing plastic food-storage bag. Mix the liquid ingredients and put them in a separate airtight container. Store the prepared mixtures in the refrigerator. Make the filling for the sausage stollen and roll it; put it on a baking sheet lined with baker's parchment and store it in the refrigerator. Make the yogurt creams and pour them into serving containers or disposable cups.

What to Pour

On *Carmelita* I have offered mimosas made with equal parts fresh-squeezed orange juice and a sparkling wine like the Brut from Washington's Chateau Ste. Michelle. But for my taste, wine in the middle of the day is far too heady; sparkling water is stimulating enough.

On the Table

Obviously, if you're on a boat, table decorations should be as simple as possible. Melissa often puts a few seashells or beach rocks on the table; these lend a nice tactile element to the dining experience. A low, unobtrusive arrangement of flowers would also be welcome. Plain white dishes and heavy plastic glasses without stems make on-board diners feel at ease; fine china and tippy glasses can be unsettling. The same rules might apply to breakfasters at a picnic table on the lawn.

ORANGE *and* CURRANT SCONES

These are my favorite scones. Some scones, like pancakes or waffles, are only good freshly baked, but these are still good a day later. The aroma of baked orange zest is a welcome wake-up call at sea or on shore.

MAKES 1 DOZEN

    2 cups flour

    2 tablespoons sugar

    2 teaspoons baking powder

    1 teaspoon baking soda

    1 teaspoon salt

    1/2 cup (1 stick) cold unsalted butter, cut into 1/2-inch bits

    1/2 cup dried currants

    1 egg

    1/2 cup fresh-squeezed orange juice

    1 tablespoon freshly grated orange zest

    Orange Glaze (recipe follows)

⊙ Preheat the oven to 400°F and line a baking sheet with baker's parchment.

⊙ In a food processor, combine the flour, sugar, baking powder, baking soda, and salt. Add the butter all at once, and process until the mixture resembles coarse crumbs. (If no food processor is available, put the dry ingredients in a mixing bowl and cut in the butter with a pastry cutter, a fork, or your fingers.)

⊙ Transfer the flour and butter mixture to a mixing bowl. Stir in the dried currants. (Dough for scones may be prepared ahead up to this point and finished just before baking.)

⊙ In a separate mixing bowl, whisk together the egg, orange juice, and orange zest. Add the egg mixture to the flour mixture, and stir just until the dry ingredients are moistened. Knead briefly to form dough, and divide the mixture in half.

⊙ On a floured work surface, shape each half into a ball and cut each ball into 6 wedges. Arrange on the baking sheet and bake for 10 to 12 minutes. Top with the orange glaze.

Orange Glaze

MAKES ½ CUP

    1 cup confectioners' sugar
    1 teaspoon freshly grated orange zest
    2 tablespoons fresh-squeezed orange juice
    1 teaspoon vanilla extract

⊙ Stir together the confectioners' sugar, orange zest, orange juice, and vanilla extract. Drizzle the mixture over the hot scones and allow to stand 5 minutes, or until glaze hardens.

SAUSAGE STOLLEN *with* POACHED EGGS *and* LEMON HOLLANDAISE

This recipe came to me from a chef who is no longer with us; I worked with him at a restaurant that closed some years ago. So I have nostalgic feelings about it. Gerald, its creator, died at a young age but left in his wake a stream of finished and unfinished recipes and works of art. We used to say he was like a supernova, constantly exploding with emotional outbursts and a passion for good food, big flavors, and constant creativity. This dish was a staple on our Sunday brunch menu. Now, wherever I make it, whether at home, in a restaurant, or on board Carmelita, *I remember Chef Gerald bouncing off the kitchen walls, arranging flowers at the last minute before we opened and yelling at me to "Pull the stollen from the oven," even as I was finishing the Hollandaise sauce or glazing the scones.*

SERVES 8

 1 pound broccoli florets

 1/4 cup (1/2 stick) butter

 1 teaspoon salt

 1 teaspoon freshly ground black pepper

 1 sheet Butter Pastry for Stollen (recipe follows) or
     1 sheet frozen puff pastry, about 10 by 20 inches

 1 pound ground pork sausage, cooked and cooled

 1 cup grated Swiss cheese

 1 egg, beaten

 8 Poached Eggs (recipe follows)

 Lemon Hollandaise (recipe follows)

⊙ With a sharp knife or in a food processor, chop the broccoli very fine. In a large sauté pan over medium-high heat, sauté the chopped broccoli

47

in the butter. Season with the salt and pepper. Spread the broccoli on a baking sheet to cool.

⊙ Put the pastry on another baking sheet lined with baker's parchment and spread the cooled broccoli over two-thirds of the sheet, leaving one long side uncovered. Spread the sausage and then the cheese over the layer of broccoli. Brush the uncovered area of pastry with some of the beaten egg.

⊙ Roll the pastry, jelly roll fashion, enclosing broccoli, sausage, and cheese and sealing the log with the egg-brushed side. Brush the top and sides of the roll with the remaining beaten egg. (The stollen may be assembled up to this point and kept refrigerated overnight.)

⊙ Preheat the oven to 400°F. Bake the stollen until it is well browned, and the filling is bubbling hot and oozing out of the ends, about 30 minutes. Let it cool on the sheet for about 5 minutes before slicing. Trim the ends, then cut into 8 diagonal slices. Serve each piece with a poached egg and 2 tablespoons of the Hollandaise sauce.

Butter Pastry *for* Stollen

MAKES A SHEET ABOUT 10 BY 20 INCHES

2 cups unbleached all-purpose flour
1 cup (2 sticks) cold unsalted butter, cut into 1/2-inch bits
1 teaspoon kosher salt
1/3 cup cold water

⊙ In a food processor, combine the flour, butter, and salt. Process just until the mixture resembles coarse crumbs; leave some chunks of butter about the size of small peas. (If no food processor is available, combine the flour and salt in a large mixing bowl and cut in the butter with a pastry cutter, a fork, or your fingers.)

◉ Transfer the flour and butter mixture to a large mixing bowl and sprinkle the cold water on top. Work the water into the flour mixture just until the dough comes together into a scrappy mass. Do not knead or overwork; it is not necessary to make the dough into a smooth ball.

◉ On a floured work surface, roll the dough into a rectangle measuring 10 by 20 inches. Fold the rectangle into thirds, like a letter, and reroll it to its former size. (The folding smooths the sheet and creates a layered effect.)

Poached Eggs

MAKES 12 EGGS

>12 cups water
>3 tablespoons vinegar
>1 tablespoon salt
>1 dozen eggs

◉ In a large sauté pan over high heat, bring the water, vinegar, and salt to a boil. Reduce heat to a simmer. Break the eggs into the simmering water one by one and cook for 4 minutes. Remove the eggs from the water with a slotted spoon and serve at once.

Note: Poached eggs are best served immediately, but if you're cooking for more than three or four people, the eggs may be poached in advance and held in a shallow baking dish filled with cold water for up to 1 hour. At serving time, lift the eggs out of the cold water with a slotted spoon and slip the eggs back into boiling water for a few seconds to reheat them.

Lemon Hollandaise

3 egg yolks
1 tablespoon fresh-squeezed lemon juice
1 teaspoon freshly grated lemon zest
1 cup (2 sticks) butter

⦿ In a food processor or in a medium mixing bowl with a whisk, combine the egg yolks, lemon juice, and lemon zest. Melt the butter in a small saucepan over high heat just until it is sizzling hot. With the food processor running or whisking constantly, drizzle in the hot butter, starting with a very thin stream and gradually working up to a steady flow.

⦿ When all of the butter has been added, the sauce may be kept warm briefly, but reheating will cause it to separate. Serve hot.

Note: If you're serving Hollandaise to a larger group and you want to prepare it ahead, you can keep the finished sauce in a vacuum bottle or an insulated coffee carafe for up to 3 hours.

YOGURT CREAMS *with* BALSAMIC STRAWBERRIES

These tangy cousins of panna cotta *are a nice alternative to prepared yogurt. If you make them in disposable cups, they can be dipped in hot water, then unmolded onto serving plates and garnished with balsamic strawberries. Or make the creams in individual serving dishes and top each one, just before serving, with a spoonful of the berries.*

SERVES 12

 2 tablespoons dry gelatin
 4 tablespoons cold water
 1 cup sugar
 2 cups heavy cream
 3 cups plain yogurt
 1 tablespoon vanilla extract
 Balsamic Strawberries (recipe follows)

◉ Spray 12 disposable 4-ounce cups with nonstick vegetable spray and set aside. In a medium saucepan, sprinkle the gelatin over the cold water and let it soften for 5 minutes.

◉ Add the sugar and heavy cream to the gelatin and cook over medium heat, stirring, until the gelatin and sugar are completely dissolved. Remove from heat and stir in the yogurt and vanilla extract. Pour the mixture into the prepared cups and chill for at least 1 hour before serving.

◉ At serving time, dip the cups in hot water, press around the edges of the cups to free the creams, and turn them out onto plates. Serve with the balsamic strawberries.

51

Balsamic Strawberries

Don't make these berries too far in advance or they will release too much of their juice.

MAKES 4 CUPS

> 2 pints strawberries
> 1/3 cup sugar
> 2 tablespoons balsamic vinegar

⊙ Cut the tops off the strawberries and rinse in cold water. Split each strawberry in half lengthwise and put them in a serving bowl. About 5 minutes before serving, toss the berries with sugar and balsamic vinegar to coat.

From Pike Place
A Dinner *to* Toast *the* Farmers Market

WHOLE WHEAT BUTTER CRACKERS

FRESH WHITE CHEESE *with* GARLIC *and* THYME

PAN-SEARED PRAWNS *in* TOMATO BUTTER *with* SPINACH FLANS

PEAR-SHAPED GAME HENS *with* CHANTERELLE
   MUSHROOM STUFFING

GREEN BEANS *and* RAINBOW TOMATOES

MARKET STALL FRUIT TART

I can't remember my first thoughts on seeing Pike Place Market; I remember only the sensations. It was in early September 1980, one of those piercingly blue-skied days when the sun was warm but the air in the shade was decidedly cool. A colorful late-summer crowd gave the place a carnival feel. Every eye was peeled, every neck was craned to take in the sights. Music wafted all around—a folk singer with a guitar at one end of the market, a lone saxophone player halfway down the stairs at the other, and a group playing Andean pan flutes somewhere in the middle. The colors of the flowers were electric, and everywhere, everywhere, was the food.

In the produce stalls, the last strawberries of the season were shoulder to shoulder with the first ripe apples. Verdant spinach was arrayed in neat rows, and exotic Asian greens tumbled from stalls piled as high as my head. The greens—new to me then, familiar to me now—were vying for my attention with wild mushrooms, brainy heads of cauliflower, and a dozen varieties of squash. Peppers too colorful and bright to be real, I thought, hung in ropes between braids of garlic and dried purple statice flowers.

Tucked behind Jack's Fish Spot, a place I have come to appreciate for fresh oysters and smoked salmon, I found Pike Place Market Creamery, a business I still frequent twenty-five years later. (It's *the* place for fresh eggs and dairy products.) I was close on the heels of a childhood friend who had been in Seattle a few years already and knew enough of the market to give me an introductory tour. My favorite cheeses, discovered in New York delicatessens and impossible to find in suburban grocery stores then, were suddenly available, and beside them were new cheeses that promised to become favorites as soon as I had time to try them.

We hurried across the street, swept up in the crowd and in the spell of this incredible bounty. Our destination was Pike Place Fish. And here, our faces cooled in the icy air, surrounded by the smell of seafood as fresh as if it had just been lifted from the waves—which, of course, it had been—we stopped. Indeed, the whole river of walking people stopped, and our heads turned in unison to see a huge salmon fly from the hands of a long-haired, white-aproned vendor into the waiting arms of another man behind the counter.

"I can't believe we got here just in time to see that," I said. But no sooner had I absorbed the dancelike motion than it happened again. And when we selected a salmon of our own, it happened yet again.

Close to 10 million people visit the market each year, making it the most popular landmark in the Pacific Northwest. A considerable number of those visitors must be as impressed as I was, and twenty-five years later, subsequent visits leave me almost equally spellbound. When my daily commute from Bainbridge Island to Canlis restaurant took me right through the market, I drove off the ferry and made my way up from the waterfront to Queen Anne Hill, passing through the famous Market Hillclimb on the way.

I often stopped there to pick up some last-minute ingredient for the restaurant, or, when I had time or needed a little inspiration to come up with specials, I would stop just to walk through the produce stalls and allow the fruits and vegetables to write new recipes for me. A cache of wild mushrooms here, a bundle of perfect haricots verts there, and a free sample of some really sweet little tomatoes might come together first at the market and later on the plate. The first local spot prawns of the season or, for that matter, the first local nectarines might demand a spot on the menu that night.

The market changes every day, and it has changed substantially over the years. But, like the friend who first showed it to me, it remains true to its essential character. Indeed, change is a vital element of that character, and it has always been part of the market's story. In the 1930s, more than six hundred farmers held permits to sell produce there, and many of them were Japanese. During World War II, at the same time that those Japanese residents were tragically moved out and interned, other farmers were called into military service or went to work in defense plants. Overnight, almost half the independent farmers were gone. The

Rainier Valley, where many of the most productive farms had been, was gradually transformed into a light industrial/warehouse district, and the market went into a decline.

Fortunately, a grassroots citizens' group, Friends of the Market, formed to help save Pike Place in the early 1970s, and its second heyday began. In the last quarter of the twentieth century many market buildings were renovated or reconstructed, and surviving businesses have gotten a boost from an influx of new stalls and new stores.

Meanwhile, neighborhoods outside the center of Seattle have hatched their own thriving farmers markets, and most Seattle chefs recognize these markets as the lifeblood of a sustainable food economy. The neighborhood farmers markets support local farmers, and healthy local farms make it possible for us to have the best possible produce in our kitchens. So here's to the farmers markets and the farmers themselves.

The Day Before

Make the cheese and chill it. Bake the butter crackers and keep them in an airtight container. Prepare the spinach flans and chill them. Make the stuffing for the hens, bone the hens, and make a broth from the bones. Prepare the crust and the filling for the tart, but don't assemble it until the afternoon of the dinner party.

On the Table

Arrange the hors d'oeuvres on a cocktail tray lined with a plain white napkin. The prawns in tomato butter could be served on a white plate or a glass one, but anything dark would make it difficult to appreciate the color of the sauce. Fairly large dinner plates should be used for the entrée. You will also need dessert plates for the tart. If you are able to shop at Pike Place Market, the flower choices are many; in other parts of the country, opt for something colorful and not too formal—tulips in the spring, sunflowers or dahlias in the summer, chrysanthemums in the fall.

What to Pour

The vegetal power of the garlic and herbs in the cheese is offset by all that butterfat, so pairing a wine with the hors d'oeuvres is a snap; sparkling wine is one option, but it's easy to pair the crackers with cocktails or with the same wine you pour for the first course. With the prawns, pour a chardonnay from Washington or a white Burgundy; you could stay with this through the main course, but a pinot noir from Oregon or a proper red Burgundy would be even better. With the tart, try a late-harvest Riesling or a sweet muscat like Essencia or Muscat de Beaumes-de-Venise.

Make It Simpler

If making your own butter crackers demands too much time, a baguette may be sliced and toasted as a vehicle for the cheese. I have also served this cheese piped into edible nasturtium blossoms. Served with a simple mound of fresh sautéed spinach instead of spinach flans, the prawns in tomato butter are still quite good. And while a boned game hen is exciting and different, the mushroom stuffing may be tucked under the skin of a free-range chicken breast with happy and more immediate results. If time is of the essence, consider buying a ready-made tart or simply serving an array of ripe fruit in season.

WHOLE WHEAT BUTTER CRACKERS

Crackers are easier to make than most people imagine. Essentially, they are very thin biscuits made with minimal leavening so that they stay relatively flat. Once you grasp the technique, myriad variations are possible—from additions of rye flour, sesame seeds, or poppy seeds to sprinkles of sea salt or cracked black pepper pressed into the dough right before baking.

MAKES 24 CRACKERS

1/2 cup whole wheat flour

1/2 cup unbleached white flour

1/2 teaspoon baking powder

1/2 teaspoon salt

1/2 cup (1 stick) unsalted butter, cut into 1/2-inch bits

3 tablespoons cold water

⊙ Preheat the oven to 375°F. In a food processor, combine the wheat and white flours, baking powder, and salt. Add the butter all at once, and process until the mixture resembles coarse crumbs. (If no food processor is available, combine the flour, baking powder, and salt in a large mixing bowl and cut in the butter with a pastry cutter, a fork, or your fingers.)

⊙ Transfer the flour and butter mixture to a large mixing bowl and sprinkle the cold water on top. Work the water into the mixture just until the dough comes together into a scrappy mass; do not knead or overwork. Chill the dough for a few minutes before rolling.

⊙ On a floured work surface, roll the dough into a rectangular sheet about 12 by 18 inches. Fold the rectangle into thirds, like a letter, and transfer it onto a nonstick silicone pan liner or a sheet of baker's parchment. Reroll the dough to its original size. (This will give the crackers a flaky texture.)

⊙ Use a pizza cutter to cut the dough into 24 bite-sized rectangles, about 1½ by 3 inches each. Move the dough onto a baking sheet, and prick each piece with a fork to prevent it from puffing up too much in the oven.

⊙ Bake crackers for 15 to 18 minutes or until puffed and golden brown. Once baked, crackers may be stored in an airtight container for several days, but they are best used within a day or two of baking.

FRESH WHITE CHEESE *with* GARLIC *and* THYME

I use "Nancy's" brand cream cheese to make this incredibly simple and delicious spread. While most packaged cream cheese contains additives, brands labeled "natural" have a softer, more appealing texture. Organic cream cheese is best.

MAKES ABOUT 2 CUPS

1 package (8 ounces) natural cream cheese
1 tablespoon chopped fresh garlic
1 tablespoon fresh thyme leaves
1 teaspoon kosher salt
1/2 teaspoon freshly ground black pepper
1/2 cup heavy cream, preferably organic

⊙ In a food processor or a small mixing bowl, mix the cream cheese with the garlic, thyme, salt, and pepper until it is smooth.

⊙ In a separate small mixing bowl, whip the cream until stiff. Fold half of the whipped cream into the cream cheese mixture and stir to loosen. Fold in the remaining cream, and stir just until combined.

⊙ Transfer the cheese to a self-sealing plastic food-storage bag, and cut off one corner to make an impromptu pastry bag. Squeeze the cheese onto butter crackers or small toasted bread rounds. Keep any unused cheese refrigerated.

PAN-SEARED PRAWNS *in* TOMATO BUTTER *with* SPINACH FLANS

Sautéed prawns should be in every cook's repertoire; they can be presented in any number of ways. Typically, the shellfish are tossed in hot oil, then finished with a splash of wine. In this version, the prawns are finished with a purée of fresh tomatoes in vinegar. The last touch is one of butter to bring the pan juices together in a smooth liaison. The spinach flans make a soothing foil to the bold-flavored prawns and provide a nice color contrast, too.

SERVES 6

18 large prawns, about 1 pound

2 ripe medium tomatoes

4 cloves garlic

1 tablespoon red wine vinegar

A few thyme sprigs, or 1/2 teaspoon dried thyme leaves

2 tablespoons olive oil

1/2 cup (1 stick) cold butter

Sea salt and freshly ground black pepper, to taste

Spinach Flans (recipe follows)

⊙ Butterfly the prawns: With a sharp knife, cut the prawns along the length of their spines so they will open when they are cooked. Rinse them to remove any dark matter, then remove the shells, leaving only the tails intact.

⊙ Quarter the tomatoes and put the wedges skin side down on a cutting board. Use the knife to scoop the insides into a blender, leaving a 1/4-inch-thick piece of skin. Cut the thick skins into 1/4-inch dice to garnish the finished dish, and set aside. In the blender, purée the insides of the tomato, the garlic, and vinegar. Purée the mixture by pulsing the blender on and off a few times, then allowing it to run uninterrupted for about 5 seconds. The goal is to crush the tomato pulp and leave the seeds relatively undamaged. Pass the purée through a strainer into a small saucepan and discard the seeds.

⊙ In a large sauté pan over very high heat, sauté the butterflied prawns and thyme in the olive oil just until the prawns are turning pink, about 2 minutes. Add the tomato mixture all at once, and swirl the mixture with the prawns until the liquid has evaporated to about half its original volume. Add the butter and swirl until it has emulsified with the liquid to form a smooth sauce. Add salt and pepper.

⊙ To serve, place a spinach flan in the center of each plate. Using tongs, arrange three prawns in a circle around each flan. Give the tomato butter a final whisk to make sure it is smooth, then drizzle it over the prawns. Sprinkle on the tomato dice and serve at once.

Spinach Flans

This is a dish that looks as though it takes more effort than it really does. Vegetable flans like this one and the Green Pea Flans served with salmon (see page 31) are a cinch to make and serve, but if you are under the gun or worried about all the cream and eggs, opt for a simple sauté of the onions, garlic, and spinach.

SERVES 6

    I large bunch fresh spinach, or one 12-ounce
        bag prewashed spinach leaves
    I small onion, thinly sliced

2 tablespoons olive oil

2 teaspoons chopped fresh garlic

1/4 cup heavy cream

1/8 teaspoon ground nutmeg

2 eggs

1 teaspoon kosher salt

1/2 teaspoon freshly ground black pepper

⊙ Preheat the oven to 375°F and butter six 4-ounce soufflé cups or ovenproof molds. Arrange the cups in a baking dish that will comfortably hold them all.

⊙ Remove the stems from the spinach and rinse the leaves in several changes of water; cut the leaves into wide ribbons and set aside.

⊙ In a large saucepan over medium-high heat, cook the onions in the olive oil, stirring regularly, until the onions are completely tender but not brown, about 5 minutes. Add the garlic, then stir in the spinach, one handful at a time; it will shrink down as it goes into the pan, making room for the next handful. Stir in the cream and nutmeg and cook, stirring, until the cream boils and the spinach is cooked through, about 2 minutes.

⊙ Transfer the cooked spinach to a blender or food processor, secure the lid, then drape a towel over the blender to prevent splashing. Purée the spinach by pulsing on and off, using short pulses at first so that the hot mixture does not overflow. Remove the lid, add the eggs, salt and pepper, and blend until smooth. Distribute the spinach custard evenly between the buttered soufflé cups.

⦿ Pour boiling water into the baking dish until it reaches halfway up the sides of the cups. Cover the baking dish with buttered baker's parchment and then with aluminum foil. Bake for 25 minutes. Serve the flans at once, or keep them warm in a 200°F oven for up to 1 hour, or refrigerate and reheat in a pan of simmering water as needed. To serve, loosen the edges of the flans with a spatula or knife, slipping the point of the spatula down the sides of the flans to let in enough air to release them. Invert onto plates and serve hot.

PEAR-SHAPED GAME HENS *with* CHANTERELLE MUSHROOM STUFFING

This dish is a variation on one originally created by René Verdon, who served as White House chef during the Kennedy era. I have simplified it considerably, but it remains a challenge to bone the game hens. If your butcher will do this part for you, it's a cinch; if not, take time to bone the birds the day before you plan to serve them, so you won't have to rush.

SERVES 6

> 3 (24-ounce) game hens
> Salt and freshly ground black pepper, to taste
> 1 pinch dried thyme leaves
> Chanterelle Mushroom Stuffing (recipe follows)
> Marsala Sauce (recipe follows)
> Thyme sprigs for garnish

⦿ If you were unable to persuade your butcher to do it for you, bone the game hens: With a sharp knife, cut along the breastbone, carefully separating the meat from the breastplate first on one side and then on the other. Disjoint first one wing and then another; cut along the backbone and disjoint each thigh. Cut out the thighbones, and leave the lower leg bones intact. The aim is to form two nearly boneless half-birds from each game hen, with only the lower leg bone attached.

⊙ Use all the bones to make a broth, cover them with water in a heavy 1-gallon stockpot and simmer gently for 1½ to 2 hours. Strain the stock and discard the bones. Spoon off the fat and boil the broth down to make 1 concentrated cup.

⊙ Preheat the oven to 350°F and sprinkle the boned half-birds with the salt, pepper, and thyme.

⊙ In each half-bird, fill the hole left from the thighbone with ¼ cup of the stuffing, and wrap breast meat over the stuffing. Fold thigh meat over breast meat and place each half-bird, seam side down, in ramekins with the one remaining leg bone pointing straight up.

⊙ Roast the birds for 35 minutes, or until they are well browned and cooked through. (An instant-read thermometer inserted into the center of each half-bird should read 170°F.) While the birds are roasting, start making the sauce, then keep the birds warm while you finish it.

⊙ To serve, on large dinner plates, arrange each half-bird on a bed of the sautéed green beans and tomatoes. Pour the sauce over the birds and serve at once, with sprigs of thyme for garnish.

Chanterelle Mushroom Stuffing

This forcemeat, designed to fill a boned hen, has such interesting texture and flavor that it practically stands on its own.

MAKES ABOUT 1½ CUPS

½ pound chanterelle mushrooms, finely chopped

2 tablespoons butter

1 slice white bread, crust removed

⅓ cup heavy cream

3 ounces white chicken meat

1 teaspoon dried thyme leaves, crushed

½ teaspoon salt

⅓ teaspoon freshly ground black pepper

1 pinch ground nutmeg

⊙ Sauté the chopped mushrooms in butter and cool. Put the bread in a small mixing bowl with the cream and allow it to soak.

⊙ In a food processor, process the chicken meat until perfectly smooth. Add thyme, salt, pepper, and nutmeg, and process to combine. Add the sautéed mushrooms and the bread soaked in cream. Pulse on and off until the mixture is smooth. (The stuffing may be made a day in advance and kept refrigerated.)

Marsala Sauce

This reduction sauce requires no special skills, but it does demand some attention. No binders or starches are used to hold the sauce together, so keeping the fat in suspension is a bit of a balancing act. If it is not reduced enough, it will be thin and runny. If it's overreduced and too much of the liquid has boiled away, the sauce will separate and the fat will float to the top. If this happens, add another splash of marsala and boil the sauce, whisking over high heat just until the sauce comes together.

MAKES ABOUT 1½ CUPS
    ½ cup marsala
    ½ cup heavy cream
    I cup concentrated broth made from reserved bones
    Pan juices from roasted game hens

⊙ In a medium sauté pan, boil the marsala until it is reduced to a thick glaze covering the bottom of the pan; be careful not to let it burn. Add the cream and the concentrated broth, and continue boiling until the sauce is reduced to about half of its initial volume.

⊙ As soon as the hens come out of the oven, pour their juices into a small saucepan or a heatproof measuring cup and tilt the pan to collect all the fat in one spot. Spoon off as much of the fat as you can, then add the remaining juices to the sauce. Whisk the sauce over high heat for about 1 minute, and serve at once over the roasted game hens.

GREEN BEANS *and* RAINBOW TOMATOES

Tiny haricots verts, the tender young green beans with the fancy French name, are one of my all-time favorite market vegetables, especially when they are paired with tiny multicolored cherry tomatoes, which are increasingly available at farmers markets and better grocery stores.

SERVES 6

6 cups water
1 tablespoon kosher salt, plus 1 teaspoon
1 pound small green beans (haricots verts)
3 tablespoons butter
1/2 teaspoon freshly ground black pepper
1 pint multicolored cherry tomatoes

⊙ Put the water and 1 tablespoon salt in a large saucepan, and bring to a boil. Meanwhile, trim the stem ends from the green beans, leaving the delicate pointed "tails" intact. Boil the green beans until bright green and just barely tender, about 3 minutes, then drain and scatter them in a single layer on a tray or a baking sheet to cool. (The beans may be prepared up to this point a couple of hours ahead and finished just before serving.)

⊙ In a large sauté pan, melt the butter over medium-high heat with the remaining salt and the pepper. Add the cherry tomatoes and cook, stirring, for 2 or 3 minutes, or until the tomatoes are blistered and warmed through; add the green beans and cook until they are heated through. Distribute the vegetables evenly between large dinner plates, and serve at once as a bed for the roasted game hens and stuffing.

MARKET STALL FRUIT TART

At the stalls of Pike Place Market, fruits arranged in neat clusters and rows constitute a feast for the eyes. With five different colors of fruit arranged on top, this tart evokes the same sense of orderly abundance, albeit on a smaller scale. In restaurant kitchens, I have assembled individual-sized tarts to order. We made the shells and the pastry cream ahead of time and assembled them at the last minute. At home, I do the same thing with one big tart. Serve this tart on a rectangular platter or on the long side of a wooden fruit box, such as a grape crate.

SERVES 6

Almond Pastry (recipe follows)
Vanilla Pastry Cream (recipe follows)
2 full-flavored peaches or nectarines
3 kiwifruits
12 small strawberries, or 6 larger ones
1 bunch "champagne" grapes or other small seedless grapes
1 half-pint raspberries
1 cup Apple Cider Jelly (optional) (recipe follows)
Mint sprigs for garnish (optional)

⊙ Prepare the almond pastry ahead of time and keep it at room temperature until just before the tart is assembled. Prepare the vanilla pastry cream and keep it refrigerated.

⊙ No more than 2 hours before you plan to serve the tart, assemble it. Spread the pastry cream on top of the almond pastry. Cut the peaches into thin slices and arrange them like shingles along one side of the tart. Peel and slice the kiwifruits and arrange the slices against the row of

71

peaches. Remove the stems from the strawberries and cut each one into a fan. Unfurl the strawberry fans along the opposite length of the tart. Remove the stems from the grapes and tumble a row of them down the length of the tart next to the strawberries. Fill in the center of the tart with a row of raspberries.

⊙ For a sparkling, finished look, melt the apple cider jelly in a small saucepan and brush it over the fruits. If you like, finish the tart with a mint sprig marking each portion. Serve in 2-inch slices.

Almond Pastry

MAKES ENOUGH FOR ONE 6- BY 12-INCH TART

1/4 cup (1/2 stick) butter
1/2 package (3 1/2 ounces) almond paste
2 tablespoons sugar
I medium egg white
I cup flour
1/4 teaspoon salt

⊙ Preheat the oven to 375°F and line a baking sheet with baker's parchment.

⊙ In the bowl of an electric mixer with a paddle attachment or in a medium mixing bowl with a wooden spoon, beat butter, almond paste, and sugar on medium speed until smooth and creamy. Add the egg white and beat until smooth. Reduce the mixing speed to low and add the flour and salt, beating just until mixture is combined.

⊙ Turn the dough out onto a floured work surface, and form it into a log with your hands. With a rolling pin, tap the log down its length to flatten it into a rectangle. Sprinkle the pastry with flour as needed to keep it sliding smoothly on the countertop and prevent it from sticking to the rolling pin. Roll the rectangle out to measure about 6 by 12 inches.

⊙ Carefully transfer the pastry to the baking sheet. Prick the pastry with a fork at regular intervals.

⊙ Bake until the pastry is brown at the edges and slightly puffed, about 15 minutes. Cool completely on the pan; then carefully move the baked pastry sheet to a rectangular tray or a piece of clean wood the appropriate size. Top with pastry cream and fruit before serving.

Vanilla Pastry Cream

MAKES 2 CUPS

3/4 cup sugar
1/4 cup cornstarch
1/2 teaspoon salt
I whole egg, plus I egg yolk
I cup whole milk
1/2 vanilla bean, split and scraped
2 tablespoons butter
I teaspoon vanilla extract

⊙ Put the sugar, cornstarch, and salt in a heavy saucepan, and whisk in the egg and the egg yolk. When the mixture is smooth, whisk in the milk and vanilla bean.

⊙ Cook the custard over medium-high heat, stirring constantly, until it begins to boil; then whisk it rapidly to prevent the formation of lumps.

⊙ When the custard has thickened to the consistency of sour cream, transfer it quickly to a mixing bowl to halt the cooking process. Remove the pieces of the vanilla bean pod. Stir in the butter and the vanilla extract. Chill the custard completely before using it as a filling for cream pies or tarts.

Apple Cider Jelly

For a fruit tart, apple jelly from a jar is fine, but homemade apple cider jelly is fun and easy to make. The technique is so simple, in fact, that it provides an excellent introduction to canning and home preserving. Serve the jelly at breakfast time with scones or toast, or use it as a topping for summer fruit tarts.

MAKES 6 HALF-PINT JARS

    4 cups apple cider
    1/4 cup fresh-squeezed lemon juice or apple cider vinegar
    1 (2-ounce) package powdered pectin
    6 cups sugar

⊙ In a stockpot or a canning kettle, cover six 8-ounce canning jars with boiling water. Simmer, covered, over low heat to sterilize jars for at least 10 minutes, or as long as it takes to make the jelly.

⊙ Put the cider, lemon juice, and pectin in a heavy, 1-gallon stockpot or Dutch oven over high heat. When the liquid comes to a boil, stir in the sugar. When the liquid boils again, set a timer for exactly 2 minutes, then take the pot off the heat.

⊙ Using tongs, lift the sterilized jars from their simmering water bath and place them empty and upright on a clean kitchen towel. Transfer the hot jelly to the jars and seal them according to the manufacturer's instructions. Dip one corner of a clean, lint-free towel into the boiling water and wipe the lips of the jars to remove any jelly.

⊙ Put the jars back into the boiling water, and boil for 5 minutes. Allow the jelly to cool in the jars, undisturbed, for several hours or overnight. Any jars that don't seal may be kept in the refrigerator; sealed jars will keep in a cool, dark place for at least a year.

Behind *the* Garden Gate
High Tea *in an* Island Garden

A PERFECT POT *of* TEA

BETSY'S BLUE CHEESE *and* SORREL SANDWICHES

SWEET BROWN BREAD

CELTIC OATMEAL SCONES

RASPBERRY JAM

BUMBLE BERRY TARTLETS

It was our honeymoon. After a couple of nights spent at a friend's rustic cabin in the tiny town of Alger near Bellingham, Washington, we moved to a tiny room in Vancouver, British Columbia, where we attended the World's Fair, which happened to be going on. Next we camped on the ocean side of Vancouver Island near the town of Tofino, and finally, we checked into the lovely old Empress Hotel in Victoria. There we washed off the salt and the camp dirt, put on fancy clothes, and went to the lobby for tea. Ever since, I have had a weakness for tea parties with little sandwiches, scones, and tartlets.

In Friday Harbor on San Juan Island, where we spent the first twelve years of our marriage, we took a lot of our meals on the lawn of a rented house on the edge of town. The house wasn't much, but the lawn commanded a sweeping view of the neighboring islands and Mount Baker beyond. There we set up a large spool abandoned by some cable layers and a few goofy old chairs. The soil was very shallow on top of the bedrock where we were perched, so our outdoor dining room was flanked by barrels filled with soil, in which we planted a few herbs and perennial flowers.

On cool spring mornings, when the moss formed a carpet underfoot, wild blue camas flowers and red Indian paintbrush surrounded our breakfast table. By early summer, sweet peas climbed the trellis beside the house, and an old rosebush opened its apricot-colored blossoms. In the barrels, Betsy's perennials, tall spikes of lupine and delphinium, were set against a backdrop of green water and deep blue sky.

Our boys, when they were toddlers, learned to stand up by holding on to the sides of the old barrels filled with herbs and flowers. They plucked the leaves and, before they could talk, learned to taste the difference between oregano and mint, rosemary and tarragon. Their wooden high chair, painted bright enamel blue when we found it at a used furniture store on one of our return trips to Victoria, was supposed to get refinished. Instead, its finish was gradually worn away by the sun and the occasional rain shower from which we failed to rescue it. Gradually it took on the patina that designers now euphemistically call "distressed."

Betsy collected old tablecloths, so many that we used a different one almost every day, and she gathered pitchers, teapots, embroidered napkins, and all sorts of trays for carrying food and tea from the kitchen to the lawn. Over the years, we accumulated an amazing variety of serving pieces that matched the high chair and made every meal outside an occasion. But our favorite meal was always afternoon tea.

And our favorite item at teatime has been, for many years, Betsy's tea sandwiches. A clever woman who has a way with sandwiches, she put together one afternoon a grilled cheese sandwich made with blue cheese and sorrel plucked from one of the barrels, and it sent us both into realms of deepest appreciation.

It was a simple thing—just a variation on a grilled cheese sandwich. But when the cheese is blue, and the sandwich is layered with shredded leaves of fresh sorrel, and when the whole thing is served with hot tea in the cool breeze of a sunny afternoon in late spring or early summer, then the world is a bright and beautiful place. And when the woman who serves it to you is the love of your life, and she smiles, and maybe even laughs a little, as you crunch through the toast and feel the sour, buttery tang of the sorrel, then you want to experience it again and again.

Without the sorrel this sandwich wouldn't be the same. The name sorrel, which basically means "sour stuff," has been loosely applied to at least three greens containing oxalic acid. Garden sorrel, also known as common sorrel, is the kind I grow. It is lance-leafed and pale green; when it's exposed to hot sunlight, its leaves become slightly bronzed around the edges. Botanists call it *Rumex acetosa.* Cooks, as far as I know, never call it that; instead they often call it French sorrel, but that moniker is better reserved for a round-leafed variety officially known as *R. scutatus*, which is for all practical purposes interchangeable with the lance-leafed kind.

A botanically unrelated third kind of sorrel, *Oxalis acetosella*, commonly known as wood sorrel, is sometimes green, sometimes variegated, and often reddish purple. When I was a kid, we called it clover, because it looks something like a shamrock, or a three-leafed clover. Lying in the grass on spring and summer afternoons, we used to pluck its leaves and eat them, savoring the tangy oxalic bite. It is used, when it is used at all, as a shade-loving landscape plant, not as a culinary herb. But whenever I enjoy one of Betsy's blue cheese and sorrel sandwiches, that feeling of freedom that came to me when I was a child in the grass comes racing back.

Tea in our family, then, is a sentimental meal, but it's not at all sad or sappy. Rather, it's playful, almost magical. These days we live on Bainbridge Island, and we have a rather large and unruly garden surrounded by deer fencing. Our view is nothing like the one we enjoyed from our old rented home in Friday Harbor; in place of Mount Baker and the San Juan Islands, we see one tiny corner of Eagle Harbor. The old spool table and the rickety chairs have been replaced with sturdy wrought iron. But the mood and spirit of our teas remain the same.

The Day Before

Check your pantry for raspberry jam, or plan to make your own; this recipe may be made successfully with frozen berries. Make the brown bread and, when it's completely cool, wrap it and tuck it away; it's almost better the day after it's baked. Each component of the bumble berry tartlets may be prepared in advance for assembly just before teatime; keep the tart shells in a cool dry place and refrigerate the lemon custard filling. The scones should really be baked just before serving, but the dry ingredients can be measured and mixed with the butter, ready to bake quickly.

On the Table

Tea in the garden is a wonderful opportunity to break out your weirdest old dishes—especially items that hold some nostalgic value for you. I have a stack of hand-painted Japanese cake plates that came to me when my grandmother died. I have no memory of her ever using them, but I think of her whenever I take them off the shelf. The need for a cream and sugar set is an open opportunity to pull out those yard-sale finds or old family heirlooms that don't often get pressed into service. Cake stands, three-tiered plate holders, and all those other funky items that serve no real function in everyday life are almost mandatory at the tea table.

What to Pour

Tea is essential. Some people appreciate teas flavored with essential oils—such as Earl Grey, which is flavored with oil of bergamot—or some of the newer fruit-flavored teas. But pure, unadulterated black tea is the best choice with the foods in this menu; it allows the flavors to stand out. If children are involved in a tea party, hot water with sugar and cream will thrill them. Certain herbal tisanes such as peppermint tea or chamomile are good too.

Make It Simpler

Tea in the garden need not be the major production that this menu implies. Even if there isn't time to prepare so many different treats, happy times can be had with a pot of tea and a substantial snack. Almost any sandwich will do. Instead of making two different tea breads, make only one, either the brown bread or the scones; of the two, the scones are faster. Instead of tartlets, serve plain strawberries with store-bought cookies.

A PERFECT POT *of* TEA

Tea is made from the dried top leaves plucked from a certain variety of Camellia sinensis. In their natural state the leaves are green, but often the leaves are crushed and allowed to oxidize as they dry, rendering them brown (for oolong) or black. Sometimes dried tea leaves are flavored with certain essential oils. Beverages brewed from herbs and flowers such as peppermint, chamomile, and hibiscus are properly termed tisanes, and they may be prepared in more or less the same way. Good water is essential to good tea; you may wish to use bottled spring water. For tea in the garden, we use a 6-cup Brown Betty ceramic teapot. We also have a small 2-cup cast-iron pot, perfect for a quick cup or two; it has a built-in strainer. Most teapots hold about 4 cups. If yours is larger or smaller, use 1 teaspoon of loose tea or 1 tea bag for every cup of water your teapot holds.

MAKES ONE 4-CUP POT OF TEA

4 cups cold water

4 teaspoons loose-leaf tea, or 4 tea bags

Lemon wedges, sugar, and milk, as accompaniments

⊙ Pour the cold water into the teakettle and bring it to a rapid boil over high heat. While the water is heating, fill a 4-cup teapot with hot tap water to warm it up. Discard the hot water and put the tea in the teapot.

⊙ As soon as the water is boiling, take it off the heat. (Boiling the water for too long reduces the amount of oxygen in the water and makes the tea "flat.") Pour the boiling water over the tea in the teapot, cover, and let stand.

◉ Depending on how strong you like your tea, you may wish to let it steep anywhere from 3 to 5 minutes. (Most teas take on a bitter edge after more than 5 minutes.) Tea bags or a tea ball can be lifted right out of the pot; if loose leaves are used, strain the tea into another warmed teapot or distribute into waiting teacups.

◉ Serve the tea very hot, with lemon wedges, sugar, and milk passed separately. If you take sugar in your tea, it is customary to put it in the cup before the tea is poured in; the motion of the incoming tea will help it dissolve. As for milk, the jury is still out on whether it should be added before or after. According to the British Standards Institute, milk should be placed in the cup first, but we Americans tend to add it after the fact.

BETSY'S BLUE CHEESE *and* SORREL SANDWICHES

With virtually no aromatic properties and a peculiarly pronounced acid tang, sorrel is unique among culinary herbs. I often say, "It looks like spinach and tastes like lemon." We use it in soup and in a sauce for salmon, but I have come to believe that its best and highest use is in these sandwiches. Crusty artisanal bread and a quality blue cheese make the best sandwiches.

SERVES 2

2 tablespoons butter

4 slices rustic white bread such as ciabatta

4 ounces Oregon Blue Cheese or another good blue

4 large leaves of garden sorrel

Freshly ground black pepper, to taste

◉ Butter one side of each slice of bread and put it, buttered side down, on a griddle or in a skillet large enough to accommodate all 4 slices. Turn on the heat to medium or medium high, and crumble the blue cheese over the bread.

◉ Stack the sorrel leaves with all the stems pointed in the same direction, and roll them lengthwise into a tight bundle. Using a sharp knife, trim off the stems and cut the bundle crosswise into ⅛-inch ribbons. (Incidentally, this cut is called a chiffonade.)

◉ Distribute the cut sorrel evenly over the cheese. Grill the sandwiches open-faced until the cheese is melted and the buttered side of the bread is browned and crisp. Sprinkle with freshly ground black pepper. Close the sandwiches and cut each one in half. Serve hot.

SWEET BROWN BREAD

Named for the French gastronome Brillat-Savarin, Savarin molds, those ubiqui-
tous ring-shaped pans once popular for jellied salads, are perfect for quick breads.
Since there is more surface area exposed to the heat of the oven, breads bake
quickly and evenly. A Bundt pan or an angel food cake pan will also work.

MAKES ONE 10-INCH RING-SHAPED CAKE

1 cup all-purpose flour

1 cup whole wheat flour

1 teaspoon baking powder

1 teaspoon baking soda

1 teaspoon kosher salt

1 cup dried currants

1 egg

$1/3$ cup brown sugar

$1/3$ cup canola oil

$1/3$ cup molasses

1 cup plain yogurt

⊙ Preheat the oven to 350°F and thoroughly butter a 10-inch Savarin mold or a ring-shaped cake pan.

⊙ In a large mixing bowl, whisk together the flours with the baking powder, baking soda, and salt. Stir in the dried currants.

⊙ In a medium mixing bowl, whisk together the egg, brown sugar, canola oil, and molasses. When these are thoroughly combined, whisk in the yogurt.

⊙ Add the egg mixture all at once to the dry ingredients, and stir just until well combined; do not overmix.

⊙ Transfer the batter to the buttered cake pan and bake until the cake is puffed on top and beginning to pull away from the sides of the pan, about 25 minutes.

CELTIC OATMEAL SCONES

Oats stand in for most of the wheat flour in these scones, and wonderful things happen as a result; they take on a satisfying nuttiness and a depth of flavor.

MAKES 1 DOZEN SMALL SCONES

2 cups quick-cooking oats
1 cup unbleached white flour
1 teaspoon baking soda
1 teaspoon kosher salt
1/2 cup (1 stick) cold unsalted butter, cut into 1/2-inch bits
3/4 cup plain yogurt or buttermilk
Jam or jelly, and ham, as accompaniments

◉ Preheat the oven to 400°F and line a baking sheet with baker's parchment.

◉ Put the oats, flour, baking soda, and salt in a food processor, and process briefly to combine. Add the butter all at once, and pulse on and off until the mixture is uniformly crumbly. (If no food processor is available, combine the dry ingredients in a large mixing bowl and cut in the butter with a pastry cutter, a fork, or your fingers.)

◉ Add the yogurt all at once to the oat mixture, and process or stir just until the dough comes together. Do not knead or overwork.

◉ On a floured work surface, divide the dough in half, and press each half into a circle about 4 inches in diameter. Cut each circle into 6 wedges, and place the wedges about an inch apart on the baking sheet.

◉ Bake until golden brown, about 10 minutes, and serve hot with jam or jelly and slices of ham, if desired.

RASPBERRY JAM

Serve this jam with scones or toast, or stir a spoonful into plain yogurt.

MAKES 5 HALF-PINT JARS

4 cups raspberries, tightly packed

1/2 cup fresh-squeezed lemon juice

4 cups sugar

⊙ In a stockpot or a canning kettle, cover five 8-ounce canning jars with boiling water. Simmer, covered, over low heat to sterilize jars for at least 10 minutes or as long as it takes to make the jam.

⊙ In a heavy, 1-gallon soup pot or Dutch oven over high heat, mash the berries with the lemon juice and bring fruit to a boil. When the fruit has come to a full, rolling boil, stir in the sugar. Continue stirring until the mixture returns to a boil; then stop stirring and insert a candy thermometer. When it registers 220°F, take the pot off the heat. If no candy thermometer is available, stir the jam with a stainless steel spoon and observe how the mixture runs off the spoon. At first it will form two distinct streams, but when it reaches the jelling point the streams will come together to form a single hanging drop.

⊙ Using tongs, lift the sterilized jars from their simmering water bath and arrange them empty and upright on a clean kitchen towel. Ladle the hot jam into the jars and seal them according to the manufacturer's instructions. Dip one corner of a clean, lint-free towel into the boiling water and wipe the lips of the jars to remove any jam.

⊙ Put the jars back in the boiling water and boil for 5 minutes. Allow the jam to cool in the jars, undisturbed, for several hours or overnight.

Any jars that don't seal may be kept in the refrigerator; sealed jars will keep in a cool, dark place for at least a year.

BUMBLE BERRY TARTLETS

The Pacific Northwest offers a greater variety of berries than any other region of the country. A single variety, such as soft, June-bearing strawberries, makes a wonderful tart for tea; but as the season rolls on and raspberries, blueberries, and finally blackberries come tumbling into season, it's fun to mix them up. There is often a window of time at the height of summer when some of each type of berry may be rounded up, and the mixture is known as bumble berries.

MAKES 6 TARTLETS

Pastry Shells for Tartlets (recipe follows)
Lemon Custard (recipe follows)
3 cups fresh summer berries (several varieties)
Lemon balm or mint sprigs for garnish

⊙ Put the shells on a serving plate and pipe the lemon custard into them. Put ½ cup of the berries in each custard-filled shell, then garnish with sprigs of lemon balm.

Pastry Shells for Tartlets

MAKES 6 SHELLS

I cup unbleached white flour
I tablespoon sugar
½ teaspoon salt
6 tablespoons (¾ stick) cold unsalted
    butter, cut into ½-inch bits
I egg white, lightly beaten

⊙ Preheat the oven to 400°F.

⊙ In a food processor, combine the flour, sugar, and salt. Add the butter all at once, and process until the mixture resembles coarse crumbs. (If no food processor is available, combine the flour, sugar, and salt in a mixing bowl and cut in the butter with a pastry cutter, a fork, or your fingers.)

⊙ Add the egg white to the flour mixture, and work the mixture by pulsing the food processor on and off, or by stirring with a fork, just until the dough comes together into a scrappy mass. Do not knead or overwork.

⊙ On a floured work surface, shape the dough into a log, and slice the log into 6 equal parts. Roll each piece of dough into a circle about 4 inches in diameter, and drape each one over the bottom of one cup of a muffin tin turned upside down. When each piece of dough has been draped over one of the cups, put the tin on a baking sheet.

⊙ Bake the upside-down tartlet shells until they are golden brown and firm to the touch, about 7 minutes. Cool the shells completely before attempting to move them off the muffin tin. The shells will be fragile, so handle with care.

Lemon Custard

While it serves here as a foil for the berries in a teatime tart, this simple lemon pudding also stands on its own as a light dessert.

MAKES ABOUT 2½ CUPS

3/4 cup sugar
3 tablespoons cornstarch
1/4 teaspoon salt
I egg
I cup fresh-squeezed lemon juice
I cup water
6 tablespoons (3/4 stick) cold butter, cut into 1/2-inch bits
I teaspoon vanilla extract

◉ Whisk together the sugar, cornstarch, salt, and egg in a large saucepan. Put the pan over medium heat and whisk in the lemon juice and water. As the mixture begins to cook, stir with a heatproof silicone spatula, scraping the sides to make sure that no dry cornstarch is left in the corners of the pan.

◉ Continue cooking the mixture over medium heat, stirring constantly, until it comes to a boil. Allow it to boil for about 30 seconds, stirring all the while. Take the custard off the heat, and whisk in the butter and vanilla extract.

◉ Put the custard in a flat baking dish so it will be spread thin to cool rapidly; chill it for an hour, or until it has completely set. Transfer the custard to a self-sealing plastic storage bag, and cut off one corner to make an impromptu pastry bag. Use the custard to fill cakes or tarts.

At *the* Beach
A Summer Picnic

|||||||||||||||||||||||||||||||||||||||||||||||||||||||||||||||||||||||||||||||||||||||||||||||||||||||||

ROSE PETAL LEMONADE

GOAT CHEESE *and* WHITE GRAPE "TRUFFLES"

FRIED BREASTS *of* CHICKEN

BUTTERMILK BISCUITS

RAINBOW COLESLAW

MARION'S BEST OATMEAL COOKIES

There is nowhere you can go without leaving someplace else, and so when I moved to Bainbridge Island to work at Canlis restaurant in Seattle, I had to leave my home in Friday Harbor on San Juan Island. At first, I resisted. I was only doing consulting work. I rewrote the menu, brought recipes, scouted purveyors, dreamt up new plate presentations, and trained the cooks. I drove my car onto a ferryboat, came to the mainland once a week, and did what I could as an absentee consulting chef. But between the ferry ride and the freeway and the waiting time for the boats, it was about a four-hour trip each way, so when the Canlises asked me to spend more time at the restaurant, I decided it was time to make a change.

But it was hard to leave Friday Harbor. I had lived and cooked there for twelve years, and for nine of those years I had written a weekly column about food. My wife, Betsy, and I were deeply involved in the little community. My two sons, Henry and Erich, had never lived anywhere else. None of us ever imagined that we might someday move away. An island, when you live on it, feels like a world apart. We sometimes joked about going to America when we went to the mainland. In Friday Harbor, there were no chain stores, no fast-food drive-ins, no freeways, no traffic lights. In many ways, it really was a world apart.

For a long time after we moved, people would ask me if I missed the island, and I'd say, "Yes, I think about it every day." I had to try hard not to think about it. If I thought too much about it, I'd start remembering one of any of a thousand things that made me miss it, and I'd wonder if I'd done the wrong thing, leaving a tiny professional kitchen with its twelve-table dining room for a big-city restaurant with more tables than I cared to count.

For about a year, whenever I felt misty or nostalgic about the island, I'd recall almost involuntarily the last night we spent together in our old Edwardian house, the hundred-year-old gabled cottage that had once belonged to the town's second mayor. It was painted orange, and the white arbor in front was draped in tumbling vines of yellow roses; the ancient apple tree out back held a tree house in its limbs, and a tiny patch of an herb garden filled one corner of the yard. I'd think about the half-imaginary view of the harbor down the hill, visible only from the sidewalk out front and from one upstairs bedroom window.

On that last night, the furniture, the backyard barbecue, the boys' bikes, and my boxes and boxes of books were packed into a rented truck in the driveway; the rooms were bare. The house was clean and empty but still held the smells and echoes of a hundred years of habitude. We ate a pizza out of the box on the floor of the kitchen. The boys drank root beer, Betsy and I drank real beer, and for some reason, we all felt blissfully happy over dinner; we laughed until we cried. Our voices rang off the empty walls and up the narrow stairs to the empty bedrooms. Before we turned in to our sleeping bags for the night, we decided to take a walk down to the harbor to check on the little aluminum boat we kept tied there, a boat we'd have to come back for later. The town was quiet and the harbor was still.

Stars blazed where the clouds parted, and lights bounced off the waves all around the dock. The other boats rocked in their slips, their masts like tall trees around us, waving in the air. When we turned to head back up, we saw the moon beginning to rise, reddish and warm, and we stopped to take it all in. Betsy and I were arm in arm. Then I noticed that Henry's little fists were balled and pressed against his eyes. I said his name and he choked back a sob.

"I don't want to go," he managed to say. I squatted beside him, and more words came pouring out. "I don't want to leave this place. It's the only place I've ever known and everyone I know lives here, and everyone who lives here knows me, and it's beautiful here. Why do we have to move?" Then the sobs overtook him, and he pressed his face against my shoulder and squeezed the sleeves of my shirt. I patted his back. Betsy was patting him too and holding onto Erich, who was leaning against her now and trying not to cry himself.

When he pulled back a little, I pulled back too and looked into his bleary blue eyes. "Henry, I am so glad that you're the kind of kid who knows how to love a place. And I'm especially glad you love this place, because it's a good place and I love it too." Then I got a little teary-eyed myself, and he let go one more sob that was almost like a sigh.

"As life goes on, God is going to show you other places, and you're going to love them, too. Because you're the kind of kid who notices things. You'll notice a lot of little things that make every place you live a little different from any other place. He made you the kind of person who can appreciate His creation, and I'm going to help you see more of it. We'll always love Friday Harbor, and we're going to learn to love other places, too." I hugged him again and prayed that what I was saying would come true, that I wouldn't live to regret leaving this beautiful town on what felt like a magical island.

The next morning we boarded the ferry with all our worldly goods and headed south toward Seattle. I said good-bye to the world that I had known, and hello to the city where Canlis loomed larger than life, with a keen sense that a new adventure had begun. Now every trip back to the San Juans is a little adventure in itself. We're happy where we are, happier in many ways than we ever were in Friday Harbor. But the place is every bit as wonderful as we knew it was when we lived there, and going back is always a joy. We usually celebrate with a picnic in one of our favorite old haunts, like Whale Watch Park.

Our picnics have ranged from easy to extreme: from simple tailgate affairs at a place called South Beach to hikes up the side of Mount Young to take in the incredible view. On the bluffs above the Strait of Juan de Fuca on the western slope of the island, orca whales swim by several times a day as they fish for salmon in the summer. Usually a big bull swims by first and then a group of middle-aged whales comes in a cluster, with a baby or two spyhopping and slapping the water with a frisky tail. The whales are enough of an event in themselves that when they're around, the picnic is superfluous, but often we have to wait for hours for the whales to appear, and sometimes they never do. So a leisurely meal in the fresh air is a great way to pass the time, and the park is equipped with big, stable picnic tables commanding one of the most spectacular views I've ever seen.

The Day Before

While this meal could be put together and served immediately in the backyard, everything can be done ahead of time and packed for the following day. Each element of the menu should be packaged separately, then packed collectively into a cooler. If the trip is a fairly short one, the cold lemonade will provide enough of a chill without the burden of extra ice. Tuck the "truffles" into an airtight box lined with baker's parchment. Wrap the cooled fried chicken breasts individually in parchment and tuck them into an airtight container. Put the slaw in a canning jar and the biscuits and cookies in separate tins.

What to Pour

The rose petal lemonade is enough for this carefree afternoon outing, but of course a few bottles of beer or a bottle of wine could be discreetly stashed in the cooler.

On the Table

A colorful sturdy tablecloth in an old-fashioned print is essential. We keep thick white paper plates, plain paper napkins, plastic flatware, and sturdy reusable plastic cups in a closet close to the door for impromptu picnics; these things are good to have on hand.

ROSE PETAL LEMONADE

The south side of San Juan Island is rich in wild rosebushes. When I was working as a chef on the island, I often gathered their petals to flavor ice cream and lemonade. Dried rose petals, available at tea shops and specialty stores, contain the same essential oils and evoke a sense of that place for me. For some reason lemonade is more thirst-quenching than water, but frozen concentrates and powdered mixes never satisfy like fresh-squeezed lemon juice does.

MAKES ABOUT 8 CUPS

I cup boiling water

¹/₄ cup dried rose petals, or ³/₄ cup fresh

I cup sugar

I cup fresh-squeezed lemon juice

Fresh rose petals (optional)

Ice to fill a 2-quart pitcher

4 cups sparkling water or club soda

◉ Pour the boiling water over the rose petals and steep for 10 minutes.

◉ Strain the liquid into a pitcher and discard the solids. Stir in the sugar and lemon juice and continue stirring until the sugar is dissolved.

◉ Put fresh petals in the pitcher if desired and fill with ice, then pour in the sparkling water.

GOAT CHEESE *and* WHITE GRAPE "TRUFFLES"

I discovered this creative hors d'oeuvre when a number of restaurateurs and winemakers from British Columbia came to Seattle to offer the press a sampling of their wares. Ian Rennie, who once ruled the range at the Empress Hotel in Victoria and then moved to a sister property near the airport, was the chef who was making them. I didn't ask for the recipe but quickly went home and imitated them; they were just as easy as they looked.

MAKES 18 PIECES

¹/₂ pound white grapes

1 log (6 ounces) fresh white goat cheese, such as Montrachet, well chilled

1 cup finely chopped toasted nuts

⊙ Rinse the grapes, remove their stems, and pat them dry.

⊙ With a sharp, wet knife, cut the chilled cheese into 18 pieces. Flatten each piece of cheese in the palm of one hand and tuck a grape in the center. Bring the cheese around the grape to enclose it and, with a circular motion, use both hands to shape the bundle into a smooth, round ball. Repeat the process with the remaining pieces and roll them in the chopped nuts.

⊙ Line a basket or a tin with grape leaves or baker's parchment; pile in the truffles. Keep refrigerated until serving time.

FRIED BREASTS *of* CHICKEN

This version of fried chicken is based on my grandfather's recipe, but while he used a whole cut-up bird, I use easy-to-handle boneless breasts. If you opt for a whole bird, you can follow the same general procedure, but allow for an extra 5 or 10 minutes' frying time. Frying more than three or four pieces at a time can cause the breading to fall off, so the chicken is fried in small batches.

SERVES 6

- 1 cup buttermilk
- 1 teaspoon hot pepper sauce
- 3 large boneless breasts of chicken, split
- 1 cup flour
- 1 teaspoon baking powder
- 1 teaspoon salt
- 1 teaspoon paprika
- 1/2 teaspoon freshly ground black pepper
- 1/2 teaspoon dried thyme leaves
- 1/4 teaspoon ground nutmeg
- Canola oil for frying

⊙ In a large mixing bowl, combine the buttermilk and the hot pepper sauce. Cut each of the chicken breasts into three strips and put the strips into the buttermilk bath. Allow the chicken to marinate in this solution for several hours or overnight.

⊙ Combine the flour with the baking powder, salt, paprika, pepper, thyme, and nutmeg. Coat the marinated chicken with the flour mixture, shaking off any excess. Put enough canola oil in a frying pan to form a layer 1 inch deep. Heat the oil to about 375°F or until a 1-inch cube of bread floats immediately to the top and sizzles.

⊙ Arrange three of the chicken strips in one layer in the frying pan. Reduce heat to medium, cover the pan, and allow to fry for 10 minutes. Remove the lid, turn the chicken, and let it fry until it is nicely browned and an instant-read thermometer inserted into the thickest part of a strip registers 160°F, about 5 minutes. (Note: If you opt to fry bone-in pieces, cook until the thermometer registers 170°F.) Repeat with the remaining pieces.

⊙ Drain the fried chicken on a cooling rack or on brown paper bags. The chicken may be served hot, or fried several hours ahead and refrigerated to be served cold.

OVEN-FRIED BREASTS *of* CHICKEN

Back in the day when my grandfather made fried chicken, people had no qualms about fried foods, but these days the whole process gives some people pause. When I determined to adapt my grandfather's fried chicken recipe to an oven-fried format, I turned to the pages of Cook's Illustrated *and found a great formula for oven-fried chicken. The editors there used crushed melba toast to give the chicken a nice crispy coat; I adapted their technique, incorporating my grandfather's buttermilk marinade and my favorite crumb coating, the Japanese-style breading mixture known as panko.*

SERVES 4

1 egg

$\frac{1}{4}$ cup buttermilk

1 teaspoon hot pepper sauce

3 large boneless breasts of free-range chicken

1 package (3$\frac{1}{2}$ ounces) panko (Japanese bread crumbs)

3 tablespoons canola oil

1 teaspoon salt

1 teaspoon paprika

$\frac{1}{2}$ teaspoon freshly ground black pepper

$\frac{1}{2}$ teaspoon ground thyme

$\frac{1}{4}$ teaspoon ground nutmeg

◉ Crack the egg into a pie pan and beat it lightly with a fork. Whisk in the buttermilk and the hot pepper sauce. Cut each of the chicken breasts into three strips, and put the strips into the buttermilk bath. Allow the chicken to marinate in this solution for several hours or overnight.

⊙ Preheat the oven to 400°F. Line a baking sheet with aluminum foil, and put a wire-mesh cooling rack or the rack from a roasting pan on top of the baking sheet.

⊙ Put the panko on a sheet of baker's parchment and crush the bread crumbs lightly with a rolling pin. Don't pulverize them completely; if they still have some crumbly texture, the chicken will end up crispier. Work the canola oil, salt, paprika, pepper, thyme, and nutmeg into the bread crumbs.

⊙ Pull the chicken strips one at a time out of the marinade with thumb and forefinger, wipe off the excess buttermilk, and lay them in the crumb mixture. Roll each piece of chicken in the crumb mixture, pressing lightly to coat; then lay the strips at least an inch apart on the rack on top of the baking sheet.

⊙ Bake until chicken is golden brown and sizzling, about 25 minutes. An instant-read thermometer inserted into the center of a strip should register 165°F.

BUTTERMILK BISCUITS

Biscuits are great hot out of the oven, but cold, they're excellent picnic fare.
Buttermilk biscuits stay tender and less crumbly.

MAKES I DOZEN 3-INCH BISCUITS

2 cups flour

2 teaspoons baking powder

I teaspoon baking soda

I teaspoon salt

$^1/_2$ cup (I stick) cold unsalted butter, cut into $^1/_2$-inch bits

$^3/_4$ cup buttermilk

⊙ Preheat the oven to 400°F and line a baking sheet with baker's parchment.

⊙ In a food processor, combine the flour, baking powder, baking soda, and salt. Add the butter and process just until the mixture is uniformly crumbly. Add the buttermilk all at once, and process just until dough comes together, forming a ball.

⊙ On a floured work surface, roll dough to $^1/_2$ inch thick. Cut with a floured, round 3-inch cookie cutter, redipping the cutter into flour between each cut. (As you cut, press the cookie cutter straight down; resist the urge to twist it. Twisting presses the edges of the biscuits together, so if you avoid doing it, your biscuits will rise higher and more uniformly.) Fold together the scraps of dough, press them back into one piece about $^1/_2$ inch thick, and cut more biscuits.

⊙ Arrange the biscuits on the baking sheet and bake for 10 to 12 minutes, or until golden brown. Serve hot or cold.

RAINBOW COLESLAW

The dark leaves of kale and red chard give this version of coleslaw an exotic look, and the perfume of sesame oil reinforces the notion that this is no ordinary slaw. The secret to success lies in cutting the greens into long, thin ribbons —
what French cooks call a chiffonade, or ribbon cut. The greens shrink a little as they marinate in the dressing.

SERVES 6

1/2 head medium-sized cabbage, about 1 pound

1 bunch tender young kale or mustard greens

1 bunch red chard

2 medium-sized sweet carrots

1 red bell pepper

1/2 medium-sized sweet onion, grated

1/4 cup rice wine vinegar

2 tablespoons sugar

2 teaspoons sesame oil

2 teaspoons kosher salt

1 teaspoon freshly ground black pepper

3/4 cup mayonnaise

⊙ Cut the cabbage in half again to make two wedges, then cut out the core from each wedge. Press each wedge, cut side down, onto a cutting board; using a very sharp knife, cut into shreds no more than 1/8 inch thick. Long, thin strips are best.

⊙ Cut the stems from the kale and chard, roll the leaves lengthwise into tight bundles, and cut them crosswise with a sharp knife to make 1/8-inch ribbons. Grate the carrots. Remove the seeds from the red pepper and cut it lengthwise into paper-thin slices.

◉ Toss the cabbage, kale, chard, carrots, and pepper in a large salad bowl. Whisk together all the ingredients for the dressing and pour it over the vegetables. Keep refrigerated until serving time.

MARION'S BEST OATMEAL COOKIES

Marion Cunningham, author of The Fannie Farmer Cookbook *and* Lost Recipes, *developed this recipe for thin, crisp oatmeal cookies. Without any egg in the dough, they are buttery and delicate, almost like oatmeal shortbread, and quite different from the chewy nut- and raisin-filled cookies many of us remember from childhood.*

MAKES 3 DOZEN

l cup (2 sticks) butter, softened to room temperature
l cup sugar
l teaspoon vanilla extract
2 cups quick-cooking oats
l cup all-purpose flour
l teaspoon baking soda
$1/2$ teaspoon salt
$1/4$ teaspoon ground nutmeg

◉ Preheat the oven to 350°F and line three baking sheets with baker's parchment.

◉ In the bowl of an electric mixer or in a large mixing bowl with a whisk, beat the butter and sugar until it is pale yellow and smooth. Stir in the vanilla extract.

⊙ In a separate large mixing bowl, whisk together the oats, flour, baking soda, salt, and nutmeg. With a rubber spatula, scrape the butter mixture into the oat mixture, and mix with a paddle or a wooden spoon until the crumbly mass comes together to form dough.

⊙ On a floured work surface, cut the dough into 12 equal pieces, then divide each piece into 3 pieces and roll the small pieces into balls. Place the balls on the baking sheets, 12 per sheet. Using your hands or the bottom of a glass dipped in flour, press the dough balls to about ¼ inch thick.

⊙ Bake the cookies, one sheet at a time, in the middle of the oven for 10 minutes. Check the cookies, and if they are golden brown around the edges, remove them from the oven; if not, bake them 1 or 2 minutes longer. Cool the cookies completely on a rack before storing.

In *the* Barn
A Summer
Harvest Dinner

||||||||||||||||||||||||||||||||||||||||||||||||||||||||||||||||||||||||||||||||||||||||||||||||||||||||||||||||||||||||||||||||||||||||||||||||

JERILYN'S COUNTRY CRACKED WHEAT BREAD

GOAT CHEESE *with* FENNEL *and* LAVENDER FLOWERS

FARMERS MARKET VEGETABLES *with* CAPER VINAIGRETTE

BRONZED ALASKA HALIBUT *with* TOMATO *and*
   TARRAGON BUTTER

CORN PUDDING

APPLES BAKED *in* PASTRY *with* APPLE JELLY SAUCE

Sometimes a shaft of light will pass through a room in such a way that the light seems to take on a tangible presence. Tiny particles drifting in the air, ordinarily invisible, are suddenly illuminated, and dark areas of the room fall away so that inanimate objects caught in the light reflect it back boldly, declaring their presence in a sentient way. It's best for the viewer if these moments occur when the surroundings are quiet or bathed in ambient sound, like the warbling of birds or perhaps the low drone of a distant airplane.

Although they can catch us unaware, moments like these never leave us that way. Rather, those moments when light demands our attention are moments that compel us toward a greater awareness, a profound sense of belonging in the world, as if the moment were provided for our own delight, or as if our perceiving it somehow brought it into being. At times I have been awake enough to dwell in moments like these, to enter into them and allow their memory to be absorbed into a kind of metaphysical file box where I can draw on them later. The same file box holds food memories, and sometimes the two kinds of memories overlap.

My friend Jerilyn Brusseau has a sheep barn on her property where sunlight often wends its way between the boards and into the center of the building in surprising ways. A baker and a peacemaker, Jerilyn founded Brusseau's Sidewalk Café and Bakery in Edmonds, Washington, in 1978, and there she developed the recipe that eventually became the formula for the world-famous Cinnabon cinnamon rolls. But Brusseau was always more than a world-class baker; in the days before the Iron Curtain fell, while she was still running that café, she founded a group called Peace Table. The organization provided opportunities for chefs from the United States and the Soviet Union to travel and work together. And later she founded an organization called Peace Trees, which continues to work in war-torn areas of Vietnam, where land mines are being removed and trees are being planted in their place.

These days, no sheep live in the sheep barn behind Jerilyn's house; instead, the barn is a combination personal retreat space and storage shed where anything too large to be stored in the house and too precious to be discarded can find a home. One thing too large to be faced every day but too precious to surrender is the lingering presence of Jerilyn's husband, Danaan Parry, who was in the process of renovating the barn when he died suddenly of a heart attack. Danaan's spirit, though wild and free and far from contained, seems to hover about the place.

Late one summer, Jerilyn invited my wife, Betsy, and me to join her in hosting a dinner in the barn to celebrate the harvest. We all pitched in to clean the space and get it ready for the guests. As we opened the doors and scrubbed the floors, things that Danaan had left behind kept turning up, and Jerilyn's memories of him worked their way into our conversation like one of those ethereal shafts of light that occasionally holds me spellbound. His memory lit the space in the very same way, endowing certain things with profound brilliance and allowing other, less important things to fade into the shadows.

During the last decade of his life, Danaan Parry had worked on conflict resolution and made profound headway. Together, he and Jerilyn had founded an organization called the Earthstewards Network, and part of their vision had been that the barn would serve as a place where people could gather to work on healing issues.

Now, Jerilyn and Betsy set a table for eighteen and covered the surface with linen tablecloths and lace. They drummed up old silverware, filled clay bowls with flowers from our gardens, polished brass candlesticks, and filled them with beeswax tapers. When they lit the candles, the afternoon sun still streamed in through the open doors and windows, and even through gaps between the boards of the barn itself. Before we were seated, a wreath of Jerilyn's cracked wheat bread was brought forth on a board piled with goat cheese that had been rolled in lavender and fennel. And as we spread the soft white cheese over the warm brown bread, I wondered if anything had ever tasted so good.

After the bread and cheese, we sat down to an array of vegetables from the farmers market, simply dressed and served on chipped green-glazed gypsy plates. Then came grilled fish and corn pudding. And for dessert we had Gravenstein apples baked in pastry, apples plucked from the tree in our own front yard.

What made that food so good? Was it the ingredients, or was it the care and attention applied to those ingredients by the cooks? Did the goodness depend on the company; was it all about the people who joined us in the barn and made those moments glow in the warmth of their appreciation? Do great food moments arise spontaneously now and then, here and there, like will-o'-the-wisps, like shafts of light between the boards of an old barn wall? Or can they be orchestrated on demand? Why does some food strike one person as good and another as simply strange?

If you ask me, I would say that each of us carries inside us a set of criteria that any food must meet in order to qualify as "good." Each of us has a metaphorical file of moments where goodness has been illuminated for us. And that arbitrary but exacting set of parameters constitutes a palate. Like a language, a palate is formed early in life. And anyone who has dined well even once not only knows what good food is, they know how good life can be, and they can claim that goodness whenever they are awake enough to bring it into focus.

The Day Before

The bread is best delivered warm from the oven to the table, but the goat cheese can be rolled in the herbs the day before. The vinaigrette may be made the day before so that assembly of the vegetable plates is quick. The corn pudding may be made ahead too and reheated just before serving. Fillet the halibut in advance and cut it into portions; follow the directions in the recipe to partially cook it several hours before serving.

What to Pour

In the barn we drank Washington chardonnay with the bread and vegetables and switched to an Oregon pinot noir with the fish.

On the Table

Better than any other flower I know, sunflowers conjure a feeling of summer in the country. When we celebrated our first harvest dinner in the barn, we had not only sunflowers but a veritable rainbow of flowers from our gardens. To evoke the mood of the barn on that magical night, I would recommend several small mismatched vases rather than one grand centerpiece.

JERILYN'S COUNTRY CRACKED WHEAT BREAD

This bread prompted so many people to say, "You should open a bakery," that Jerilyn Brusseau eventually did, to great acclaim. She also pioneered many of the chef-to-farmer connections that characterize the contemporary Pacific Northwest food scene. For our dinner in the barn, she brushed the loaf several times near the end of its baking time with melted butter, which softened the crust and gave it a deep bronze patina.

MAKES 1 LARGE WREATH

1$\frac{1}{2}$ cups coarsely cracked wheat

1$\frac{1}{2}$ cups boiling water

1 cup warm water

6 tablespoons honey

2 packages active dry yeast

1 cup milk

1 tablespoon salt

$\frac{1}{4}$ cup ($\frac{1}{2}$ stick) butter

4 to 4$\frac{1}{2}$ cups unbleached white flour, divided

3 cups whole wheat flour

1 tablespoon canola oil

Additional $\frac{1}{4}$ cup ($\frac{1}{2}$ stick) butter (optional)

⊙ Put the cracked wheat in a small mixing bowl and pour on the boiling water. The cracked wheat will soften up a little and absorb most of the water. Let it soak until it's cool enough to touch, about 15 minutes.

⊙ Fill a large mixing bowl with hot tap water to warm it up, then pour out the hot water and put the cup of warm water in the bowl. Stir in the honey, then sprinkle on the yeast and stir until it dissolves.

⊙ Let this mixture stand, undisturbed, for 5 minutes. Meanwhile, put the milk in a saucepan over medium-high heat and cook until the milk is steaming hot. Take the pan off the heat and whisk in the salt, butter, and 2 cups of the white flour. Touch the mixture to check the temperature. It should be warm, about the temperature of a warm bath or a baby's bottle; if it's too hot to keep your finger in it, let it cool further.

⊙ Stir the milk mixture into the yeast mixture. Add 2 more cups of the white flour, 1 cup at a time, stirring well with a wooden spoon between each addition. Add the whole wheat flour in the same way, and as the dough becomes too stiff to stir, start working in the flour with your hands.

⊙ Work in the presoaked cracked wheat and turn the dough out onto a floured work surface. Knead the dough, pressing and folding it until it is smooth and elastic, sprinkling on additional white flour if needed to keep the dough from sticking to the counter.

⊙ Rub the inside of the bowl in which the dough was mixed with the canola oil. Put the kneaded dough in the bowl, and turn it over once so that the whole ball of dough is lightly coated with the oil. Cover the bowl with a damp, lint-free kitchen towel or a piece of plastic wrap, and put it in a warm place until the dough is doubled in size, about an hour.

⊙ Press the air out of the dough and let it rise until it has doubled again, about 30 minutes. Divide the dough into 3 equal pieces and roll each piece into a rope about 18 inches long. Braid the three strands of

115

dough and shape the braided dough into a circle, tucking the ends into the ring to hide where it begins and ends.

⊙ Preheat the oven to 375°F. Put the braided ring on a pizza pan or a baking sheet that has been sprinkled with whole wheat flour, and let it rise while the oven is preheating, about 30 minutes.

⊙ Bake the bread ring in the center of the oven until it is golden brown and baked through, about 40 minutes. If you wish, melt the additional butter in a small saucepan and brush the loaf with it once or twice, near the end of its baking time, then put it back in the oven. When the loaf is ready, it will make a hollow sound when it's tapped; an instant-read thermometer inserted into the center of the loaf will register about 195°F.

⊙ Present the loaf on a platter, and fill the center of the ring with rounds of the goat cheese rolled in herbs, or with a pot of the fresh white cheese from "A Dinner to Toast the Farmers Market" (see page 55).

GOAT CHEESE *with* FENNEL *and* LAVENDER FLOWERS

To my mind, artisanal goat cheeses, often found in Pacific Northwest farmers markets—and those in other parts of the country—herald the ever-expanding horizons of taste available to us. Not so long ago, cheeses like these were available only as imports. Now they serve as tangible and flavorful symbols of our American culinary renaissance. Rolled in fresh fennel and lavender flowers, a soft white goat cheese becomes an exciting centerpiece for a gathering.

SERVES 6

    2 logs soft white goat cheese, 3 ounces each

    2 tablespoons fresh fennel flowers or crushed fennel seeds

    2 tablespoons fresh or dried lavender flowers

⊙ Roll the goat cheese in the flowers, pressing firmly so that the flowers will adhere to the cheese. Serve with warm bread.

117

FARMERS MARKET VEGETABLES *with* CAPER VINAIGRETTE

In a casual home setting, an assortment of vegetables from the farmers market with a good dressing like this one is almost a meal in itself. Served with a warm loaf of good bread and a round of goat cheese, it is indeed a meal in itself, but for a celebratory summertime gathering of friends, it makes a stunning opener for a multicourse meal.

SERVES 6

> 2 pounds fingerling potatoes
> 6 cups water
> I tablespoon salt
> 2 pounds thin green beans
> 2 pints sweet cherry tomatoes
> I fresh fennel bulb, sliced thin, leaves reserved
> Caper Vinaigrette (recipe follows)

⊙ Put the potatoes, water, and salt in a large saucepan and bring to a boil. Cook the potatoes until they are fork-tender, about 10 minutes, then lift them out of the water using a slotted spoon and scatter them over a baking sheet to cool.

⊙ While the potatoes are cooking, trim the stem ends from the green beans, but leave the tapered "tails" intact. When the potatoes come out of the boiling water, drop the beans in and boil them just until they turn bright green and are barely tender, 3 to 5 minutes, depending on their size. Drain the beans and scatter them over a baking sheet to cool slightly and halt the cooking process.

⊙ Distribute the potatoes, beans, tomatoes, and sliced fennel evenly between serving plates. Decorate each plate with a few of the feathery fennel leaves, drizzle a generous tablespoon of the caper vinaigrette over each serving, and serve at room temperature.

Caper Vinaigrette

Serve this vinaigrette with cooked vegetables or on salad greens. Refrigerated, it keeps for several weeks.

MAKES ABOUT 3/4 CUP

    2 tablespoons white wine vinegar
    1 tablespoon chopped fresh garlic
    1 tablespoon stone-ground mustard
    1 teaspoon kosher salt
    1/3 cup olive oil
    2 tablespoons capers, drained

⊙ Put all the ingredients in a jar with a close-fitting lid and shake until well combined. Serve at once, or keep refrigerated until serving time.

BRONZED ALASKA HALIBUT *with* TOMATO *and* TARRAGON BUTTER

Pan-searing halibut affords a cook the most flexibility of any method I know. The halibut can be prepared well in advance up to a point and finished without any fuss, just before serving. An aromatic coating of sugar, smoked paprika, and salt provides not only a flavor boost but also a catalyst for caramelization on the delicate surface of the fish exposed to the hot oil in the pan.

SERVES 6

6 halibut fillets, about 8 ounces each

2 tablespoons sugar

I tablespoon smoked paprika

2 teaspoons fine sea salt

1/2 teaspoon ground white pepper

4 tablespoons canola oil

Tomato and Tarragon Butter (recipe follows)

⊙ Rinse the fillets and pat them dry. Mix the sugar, paprika, sea salt, and white pepper, and sprinkle the fillets with this mixture.

⊙ Over medium-high heat, preheat a large skillet for 1 minute. Put the canola oil in the pan; it should be almost smoking hot.

⊙ Put the halibut in the pan skin side up, reduce heat to medium, and allow the fish to cook, undisturbed, until a crisp brown crust has formed on the underside, about 4 minutes.

⊙ Use a flexible steel fish spatula or a pancake turner to lift the fillets out of the pan, being careful not to tear the delicate crust that has formed. Turn the fillets and place them on an ungreased baking sheet.

(The fish may be prepared ahead up to this point and kept refrigerated for several hours.)

⊙ Preheat the oven to 400°F. Bake the partially cooked halibut fillets until they are cooked through, about 7 minutes. The skins will stick to the baking sheet, so you can lift the fillets off the sheet while leaving the skins behind.

⊙ To serve, place a pan-seared fish fillet in the center of each serving plate. Top with the tomato and tarragon butter and the garnishes from that recipe (tomato dice and sprigs of tarragon).

Tomato *and* Tarragon Butter

Like the lemon butter that's served with asparagus in "A Feast for Spring," this sauce is a variation on beurre blanc, a classic French butter sauce that derives its supple texture from a technique that prevents hot butter from breaking down into clear fat and whey. The butter is held in suspension by whisking it into a flavorful liquid base—in this case, a fresh tomato purée boiled with red wine and seasonings.

MAKES ABOUT 1 CUP

2 ripe medium tomatoes (about 1/2 pound)
2 teaspoons tomato paste
1/2 cup red wine
2 cloves garlic
1 teaspoon kosher salt
1/2 teaspoon freshly ground black pepper

1 teaspoon dried tarragon leaves, or 1 tablespoon fresh
³/₄ cup (1¹/₂ sticks) butter
Tarragon sprigs for garnish

⊙ Quarter the tomatoes and put the wedges skin side down on a cutting board. Use the knife to scoop out the inside from each wedge, leaving a ¼-inch-thick piece of skin. Cut the thick skins into ¼-inch dice to garnish the finished dish, and set aside.

⊙ Put the insides of the tomatoes into a blender along with the tomato paste, red wine, garlic, salt, and pepper. Purée the mixture by pulsing the blender on and off a few times, then allowing it to run uninterrupted for about 5 seconds. The goal is to crush the tomato pulp and leave the seeds relatively undamaged.

⊙ Pass the purée through a strainer into a small nonreactive (stainless steel or enamel) saucepan and discard the seeds. Add the tarragon and bring the purée to a boil over high heat, and allow it to reduce to about a third of its original volume.

⊙ Whisk the butter into the tomato purée, and serve the tomato butter over fish. Garnish with the tarragon sprigs and tomato dice.

CORN PUDDING

Homey and comforting, corn pudding is a kind of vegetable flan. Since it is such a simple dish with no exotic flavors to hide behind, the pudding benefits greatly from careful selection of ingredients. From a local farmers market, choose the best and sweetest corn you can find. Organic butter, milk, and cream tend to have better flavors than conventionally produced dairy products. Serve the pudding hot as a side dish with fish or pork, or as a simple main dish for a casual lunch.

SERVES 6

    2 eggs
    I teaspoon kosher salt
    ¹/₂ teaspoon freshly ground black pepper
    I cup whole milk
    I cup heavy cream
    6 large ears of sweet corn

⊙ Preheat the oven to 350°F and liberally butter a 9- by 13-inch baking dish.

⊙ In a large mixing bowl, whisk the eggs together with the salt and pepper, then whisk in the milk and cream.

⊙ Trim the base of each ear of corn to make it stand flat on a cutting board. Working with one ear at a time, use a sharp knife to cut the kernels off each ear. Add the kernels to the egg mixture.

⊙ After the kernels have been cut from the ears, use the dull side of the knife blade to scrape down the ears and press out any juices clinging to them. Stir the juices into the egg mixture.

⊙ Transfer the pudding to the buttered baking dish and bake for 35 minutes, or until the pudding is browned on top and smells faintly of popcorn; it should jiggle when the dish is moved briskly back and forth. Serve hot.

APPLES BAKED *in* PASTRY *with* APPLE JELLY SAUCE

Many of the apples that are commercially grown in Washington State are kept chilled in warehouses where oxygen is replaced with nitrogen. Thanks to this high-tech storage system, remarkably fresh-tasting apples are available year-round, but certain types of apples, especially the varieties that ripen early in the summer, do not hold up well, even in these idealized conditions. These apples, with their fleeting crisp-tender texture and their flowery aroma, must be enjoyed at the height of their season. For this recipe, my favorite apple is the fragrant but sometimes elusive Gravenstein, a variety that ripens in August. If it cannot be found, consider the widely available and very agreeable Jonagold.

SERVES 6

6 medium baking apples, such as Gravenstein or Jonagold,
about 3 pounds

Filling

1/4 cup (1/2 stick) butter, softened to room temperature
1/2 cup brown sugar
2 tablespoons flour
1 tablespoon ground cinnamon

Pastry

11/2 cup flour
1/2 teaspoon kosher salt
3/4 cup (11/2 sticks) cold unsalted butter, cut into 1/2-inch bits
5 tablespoons cold water
Apple Jelly Sauce (recipe follows)

◉ Preheat the oven to 350°F and line a baking sheet with baker's parchment.

◉ Peel the apples. Use a special coring tool or a paring knife to carve the core out of each apple while leaving it whole. Put the peels and the cores in a medium saucepan and set aside.

◉ Combine all the ingredients for the filling and divide it into 6 equal parts. Press the mixture into the hollowed-out apples and set aside.

◉ To make the pastry, put the flour and salt in a food processor. Add the butter all at once, and pulse on and off just until the mixture resembles coarse crumbs; leave some chunks of butter about the size of small peas. (If no food processor is available, put the flour and salt in a mixing bowl and mix in the butter with a pastry cutter, a fork, or your fingers.)

◉ Transfer the flour and butter mixture to a large mixing bowl and sprinkle the water over the top. Work the water into the mixture just until the dough comes together into a scrappy mass. Do not knead or overwork; it is not necessary to make the dough into a smooth ball.

◉ On a floured work surface, divide the dough into 6 equal pieces and roll each piece into a 6-inch circle. Wrap each apple in a piece of dough, crimping the edges around the top. Place the apples on the baking sheet.

◉ Bake until the apples are tender, the pastry is lightly browned, and the filling is bubbling hot, about 35 minutes.

◉ Serve the apples in a pool of the apple jelly sauce.

Apple Jelly Sauce

Peels and cores from the apples
1¹/₂ cups water
2 tablespoons fresh-squeezed lemon juice
1 cup sugar

⊙ To make the sauce, cook the apple peels and cores in the water in a medium saucepan over high heat for 10 minutes, or until the apple parts are mushy. Strain the liquid into a clean saucepan and discard the solids. Add the lemon juice to the liquid used to cook the peels and cores, and cook over high heat until the mixture is boiling rapidly. Add the sugar and cook for 5 minutes longer or until the sauce is slightly thickened.

After *the* Cider Bash
A Feast *for* Autumn

ROMAINE *and* APPLE SALAD *with* TOASTED WALNUTS *and*
   OREGON BLUE CHEESE

CIDER-BRINED PORK CHOPS *with* TART CHERRY CHUTNEY

KABOCHA SQUASH FLANS

MUSTARD GREENS *with* MUSTARD SEEDS

WILLIE'S APPLE CRISP

CINNAMON ICE CREAM

Apples are inherently nostalgic. Every year when apples are ripening on my trees—tiny Lady apples, fragrant Gravensteins, hard green pippins of no particular variety, and a couple of antique varieties that might be Cornish Gilliflowers and Golden Russets—I feel inexplicably wistful. The trees are probably as old as my house, which was built in 1904, and even the people who lived here before me couldn't tell me what they were.

Perhaps their very anonymity has something to do with the way I feel about these old apples. Or maybe I feel sentimental because they ripen at the end of the growing season, when even the warmest and sunniest days are tinged with reminders of autumn—yellowing poplars across the way, Canada geese calling out their low notes and pulling themselves into V-formations to fly south for the winter. But the solemnity that reigns in my little orchard when the apples ripen is also an annual reminder of a local tradition known as the cider bash. And in contrast to my own plaintive feelings about the apple harvest, these occasions are always festive. Some local person in possession of a cider press will host an event where attendees bring boxes of their own apples to be pressed and empty jars to be filled with cider.

At one old farm here on Bainbridge Island, the ancient trees are almost crowded out by the encroaching forest, but they continue to bear good fruit; and every fall, families gather to collect it and press it into juice. Tarps are laid out under the trees, and some of the more agile members of the group climb up to shake the limbs. The fruit falls to the earth; children scream and giggle and run away to avoid getting pummeled with apples.

In the clear October light, when all the apples have been fed to the press and the amber cider flows like honey against a backdrop of city, sea, and sky, we unpack picnic lunches on the grass and drink the cider in great quaffs. The cider is sweet, but the best batches also have a bracing, bitter edge, as if in every sip one could taste the passage of time, the tenacious grasp we have on life, the disappearance of traditions like this one.

One year, within a week or two of a cider bash, Gwenyth Bassetti, the founder of Seattle's Grand Central Bakery, sent me a box of apples from her orchard near Sunnyside, in south-central Washington. "We call them Big Bumpies," she said. The name was fitting. Each apple, no two of them quite the same, weighed in at well over a pound apiece, and the scent they gave off reminded me of yellow roses. They were green and red and wonderfully misshapen. I fell in love with them at once.

Like the apples at my house, and like a lot of backyard fruit for that matter, Bassetti's Big Bumpies are of vague origins. They were discovered at the boyhood home of Gwen's husband, Fred, in a town that used to be known as Forester and is now a part of Tukwila.

"My father bought a piece of land there in 1918, one year after I was born," Fred Bassetti once told me. "Another house had been there before, but it had burned down. Still, there was a garden there and a little orchard. We had Gravensteins and Yellow Transparents and these big, bumpy apples that ripened late. No one knew what they were, but they're sweet apples and crisp, and everybody seemed to like them. I used to give scions, or cuttings, to friends all the time who wanted to grow this apple for themselves." In the 1950s, a friend of Bassetti's persuaded him to take cuttings and start a small orchard of Big Bumpies. "In 1992," said Fred, "we took some scions from his trees and started about eighty trees of our own, and a couple years after that, we planted another forty."

Most apple trees are grown in more or less the same way. Since apples do not grow true from seed, orchardists take scions from trees that bear good fruit and graft the branches onto reliable rootstock. The apples produced by these trees are virtual clones of the fruit of the trees from which they were taken. The technique has its advantages. In an orchard where all the trees are the same, all the fruit ripens simultaneously and can be harvested at once.

A field full of wild apple trees, each one grown from seed, would present serious challenges to a farmer. The early-ripening varieties would have to be picked first and the late ones would have to wait. Some sweet ones might be good for the table, but others would be good only for the cider presses. Worst of all, most of the apples would be, in the eyes of many people, good for nothing. Bitter, hard, mealy, or bland, most apples grown from seed bear little resemblance to favored varieties that have been carefully selected and cloned for hundreds, even thousands of years.

But fields full of identical, cloned apple trees bearing sweet fruit are not the utopian dream they might appear to be, either. In *The Botany of Desire,* Michael Pollan addresses the lack of diversity in modern apple farming. "The modern history of the apple—particularly the practice of growing a dwindling handful of cloned varieties in vast orchards—has rendered it less fit as a plant, which is one reason modern apples require more pesticide than any other food crop."

Apples and their predators evolve side by side; the apples that happen to have some resistance to pests survive, and the pests that have some way to overcome the resistance survive to give them fits. Apples that are particularly pretty or sweet have the advantage of attracting human defenders like us. And while it may seem that we have settled into a comfortable rut of planting only a dozen or so varieties and preserving them with sprays, new varieties are emerging all the time.

While many new varieties are fortuitous accidents, some new apples are born from a deliberate effort by growers to cross varieties with desirable characteristics. Fuji, one of the most successful new varieties in decades, was bred more deliberately, at a Japanese research station where growers crossed two old American varieties, the Red Delicious and the Ralls Janet, a favorite of Thomas Jefferson. Pink Lady, another new variety that shows a lot of promise, was developed in a breeding program in western Australia. It's a cross between a Golden Delicious and a Lady Williams.

Sometimes an apple falls to the ground, one of its seeds takes root, and somehow it doesn't get mowed down or pulled out. The Red Delicious started out that way. Originally known as the Hawkeye, it sprang up during the mid-nineteenth century on the farm of one Jesse Hiatt in Peru, Iowa, and was on the market by 1874. Cameo, a new apple that's something of a darling among Washington apple growers, originated from a chance seedling in the Wenatchee River Valley.

All the apples produced commercially these days are grown for sweet flavor and crisp texture, but many of the old varieties were grown because they made good cider, even if they weren't great to eat. I have come to believe that a few of the oddball apples in my yard were selected for cider, and so each fall I try to build a menu around apples and cider. With apples in the first course, apples in the second, cider in the marinade, cider in the glass, and apples for dessert, these menus always make me happy.

The Day Before

The salad in this menu is one I have often carried to potlucks; it's a great "do-ahead." Make the vinaigrette, toss it with the sliced apples, and put the mixture in a quart-sized canning jar; the apples will be preserved in the vinaigrette for a while. Wash and spin the lettuce and tuck it into an airtight bag, ready to toss. As for the pork chops, once they are resting in their cider-flavored brine, cooking them takes only a few minutes. The squash flans can be made ahead and reheated while the chops are cooked. The cherry chutney can be made several days ahead. As for the apple crisp, I make the topping ahead and store it in freezer bags.

What to Pour

Apple cider, fresh or hard, is probably the ideal beverage for this menu, but it lends itself readily to wine as well. For lovers of white wine, a pinot gris, especially one made in the Alsatian style, would be excellent.

Red lovers should consider a pinot noir—either a true Burgundy or a Burgundy wannabe from Oregon.

On the Table

Since apples are so beautiful, who needs flowers? Simply scatter the fruit down the center of the table in wild profusion. But be sure to rinse and refrigerate the apples later; they do not hold up well at room temperature.

Make It Simpler

In spite of its generous proportions, this meal is fairly simple to prepare. If the flans seem like too much bother, simply serve steamed squash, mashed with a little butter, salt, and pepper.

ROMAINE *and* APPLE SALAD *with* TOASTED WALNUTS *and* OREGON BLUE CHEESE

Oregon Blue Cheese is actually a brand of blue cheese that comes from the Rogue River Valley Creamery. A crumbly white cheese with bold blue-green veins, it is more like Maytag Blue or Roquefort than like the creamy soft Danish blue or the pale yellow Shropshire or Gorgonzola blue cheeses.

SERVES 6

3 large, ripe Jonagold or other crisp, sweet apples, about 1½ pounds
Apple Cider and Walnut Vinaigrette (recipe follows)
2 hearts of romaine lettuce, washed, spun dry, and cut into 2-inch pieces
6 tablespoons Oregon Blue Cheese, crumbled
Toasted Walnuts

⊙ Core the apples, then cut them lengthwise into matchsticks, about ¼ inch thick. In a large mixing bowl, combine the apples with ¾ cup of the apple cider vinaigrette, and toss to coat. Add the lettuce and toss again. Most of the apples will settle to the bottom of the bowl.

⊙ Distribute the dressed lettuce and the dressed apple matchsticks evenly between 6 chilled salad plates.

⊙ Over each salad, crumble a tablespoon of blue cheese and then scatter a generous tablespoon of toasted walnuts. Serve at once.

Apple Cider *and* Walnut Vinaigrette

For a light entrée, try tossing this salad dressing with mixed greens and topping it with the Goat Cheese Fritters (page 10). The dressing keeps refrigerated for at least a week.

MAKES ABOUT 2 CUPS

- ¹/₂ cup apple cider
- ¹/₂ cup apple cider vinegar
- 2 tablespoons sugar
- 2 teaspoons salt
- 1 teaspoon freshly ground black pepper
- ³/₄ cup walnut oil

⊙ In a small saucepan, boil the apple cider over high heat until it is reduced to about half of its original volume; it will be like a thick syrup. Remove the pan from the heat, add the cider vinegar, and swirl.

⊙ Whisk in the sugar, salt, and pepper. Then gradually whisk in the walnut oil to create a smooth emulsion. Keep the dressing chilled until serving time.

CIDER-BRINED PORK CHOPS *with* TART CHERRY CHUTNEY

A brine helps makes pork more tender and juicy. The addition of apple cider vinegar serves as an additional tenderizer and flavor booster. Don't worry about all the salt in the brine; most of it gets discarded anyway.

SERVES 6

2 cups water

1/4 cup kosher salt

1/4 cup brown sugar

1 teaspoon whole black peppercorns

6 thyme sprigs, or 1 teaspoon dried thyme leaves

4 cloves garlic, crushed

2 cups apple cider

1/4 cup apple cider vinegar

6 thick-cut bone-in pork chops, about 10 ounces each

1/2 cup olive oil

Tart Cherry Chutney (recipe follows)

⊙ Several hours before you plan to serve the pork chops, make the brine. Bring the water to a boil. Stir in the salt, brown sugar, peppercorns, thyme sprigs, and garlic and let the mixture steep for 20 minutes. Stir in the apple cider and the apple cider vinegar. Chill the brine until it is cold, about 30 minutes, then add the chops. The chops and brine can be held in a heavy-duty, self-sealing plastic freezer bag or in a nonreactive (glass or enamel) baking dish covered with plastic wrap. Allow the chops to soak in the cold brine in the refrigerator for at least 2 hours or for as long as 24 hours.

⊙ Thirty minutes before serving, preheat the oven to 350°F. Remove the chops from the refrigerator and discard the brine. Put the olive oil in a large sauté pan over medium-high heat and sear the chops, three at a time, until they are well browned, about 5 minutes on each side. Discard any olive oil remaining in the pan.

⊙ As the chops are browned, transfer them to a baking dish. Bake them until an instant-read thermometer inserted into the thickest part of a chop registers between 145°F and 150°F, about 10 minutes. Serve hot with the tart cherry chutney.

Tart Cherry Chutney

Studded with dried tart cherries, this chutney sparkles as if it were made with semiprecious stones. The vinegar causes a chemical reaction that brightens the red of the onion and the cherries, and the sugar is rendered into a shiny glaze. The chutney's bright, tangy flavor is an excellent foil to the richness of pork chops or a pork roast.

MAKES ABOUT 2 CUPS

2 cups dried tart cherries

I small red onion, thinly sliced

1½ cups apple cider vinegar

1½ cups sugar

I tablespoon salt

⊙ Put the cherries in a large, heavy, nonreactive (stainless steel or enamel) saucepan along with the red onion, vinegar, sugar, and salt. Cook over high heat, stirring, until the sugar is dissolved and the mixture is just beginning to come to a boil.

⊙ Cover, reduce heat to medium-low, and cook until the onions are tender and the cherries are plump and tender, 10 to 15 minutes.

⊙ Chutney may be served at once or kept, covered and refrigerated, for several days.

KABOCHA SQUASH FLANS

A savory custard, this side dish provides a circle of gold on a dinner plate that is as visually appealing as it is delicious. Since the flans are very soft, I always serve them with a second vegetable that has some texture, like the sautéed mustard greens that follow.

SERVES 6

½ medium kabocha squash, about 1 pound

2 tablespoons unsalted butter

½ medium white or yellow onion, thinly sliced

½ cup heavy cream

3 eggs

1 teaspoon kosher salt

⊙ Preheat the oven to 375°F and butter six 4-ounce ramekins or glass custard cups. Place the cups in a baking dish that will comfortably hold them all.

⊙ Cut the squash into disks or wedges and scrape out seeds, then cut away the peel. Cut the peeled and seeded squash into 1-inch dice. You should have about 2½ cups of diced squash.

⊙ In a large skillet or saucepan, melt the butter over medium-high heat and cook the onion for 5 minutes, or until tender and golden brown, stirring often. Add the cream and squash, bring the mixture to a boil, cover, and reduce heat to low. Let the squash simmer gently for 15 minutes, or until tender.

⊙ In a blender or food processor, combine the eggs with the salt. Pulse on and off until smooth; then add the squash mixture. Secure the lid and drape a kitchen towel over the top of the blender to prevent splashing. Pulse the squash mixture until smooth, using short pulses at first so that the hot mixture does not overflow. Distribute it evenly between the ramekins.

◉ Pour boiling water into the baking dish until it reaches halfway up the sides of the ramekins. Cover the baking dish with buttered baker's parchment and then aluminum foil. Bake until the flans are set and no longer jiggle when the ramekins are tapped, about 25 minutes. Remove the flans from the oven and allow them to stand for 10 minutes.

◉ Serve the flans at once, or keep them warm in a 200°F oven for up to 1 hour, or refrigerate and then reheat as needed. To serve, loosen the edges of the flans with a spatula or knife, slipping the point of the spatula down the sides of the flans to let in enough air to release them. Invert onto plates and serve hot.

MUSTARD GREENS *with* MUSTARD SEEDS

Heating mustard seeds causes them to pop like popcorn, so be careful when you add them to the hot oil. As soon as the greens are added, the popping stops. Like spinach, mustard greens cook down considerably, so what looks like a large amount is actually just enough.

SERVES 6

2 bunches of mustard greens, each about I pound

3 tablespoons olive oil or canola oil

I tablespoon whole brown mustard seeds

I teaspoon kosher salt

⊙ Rinse the mustard greens and shake off the water. Roll the stack of leaves lengthwise into a tight bundle. Cut the bundle crosswise with a sharp knife, into ¼-inch ribbons (what French cooks call a chiffonade).

⊙ Put the olive oil in a large sauté pan over medium-high heat and when the oil is smoking hot, add the mustard seeds. They will start to pop. Immediately add the greens, and the popping will settle down.

⊙ Move the greens quickly around the pan with tongs for 2 minutes and sprinkle them with the salt. As soon as the greens are wilted and heated through, serve them hot.

WILLIE'S APPLE CRISP

Now fully grown and starting a family of his own, Willie was a child of ten when he developed this formula for the crispest of crisps. Willie's neighbor, Sharon Kramis, a cooking teacher and cookbook author, introduced the crisp to her friend Marion Cunningham, who saw to it that the formula was widely popularized. In the late summer, I sometimes mix up a large batch of the topping mixture and keep it covered in the freezer. A windfall of berries or apples may then be quickly put to good use under a handful of the crunchy cookielike topping.

SERVES 6 TO 8

Topping

    I cup flour

    I cup sugar

    I teaspoon baking powder

    I teaspoon kosher salt

    I egg

Filling

    6 cups apples, peeled and sliced thin

    1/2 cup sugar

    2 tablespoons flour

    1/2 cup (I stick) butter, melted

    Cinnamon Ice Cream (optional) (recipe follows)

⊙ Preheat the oven to 375°F and have ready an unbuttered 8- by 8-inch baking dish.

⊙ Make the topping: Stir the flour, sugar, baking powder, and salt in a large mixing bowl. Make a well in the center of the dry ingredients and add the egg. Beat the egg with a fork and gradually incorporate it into the flour-and-sugar mixture.

⊙ Make the filling: Put the apples into the baking dish, and toss with the sugar and flour.

⊙ Sprinkle the topping evenly over the filling. Drizzle the melted butter evenly over the top. Bake until the topping is golden brown, about 40 minutes. Serve warm with the cinnamon ice cream.

CINNAMON ICE CREAM

With a deep, warm note of spice, this simple ice cream makes any dessert more memorable. It's especially good with fruit crisp and pies, but don't hesitate to serve it beside a slice of chocolate cake.

MAKES ABOUT 6 CUPS

    2 cups milk

    3 tablespoons ground cinnamon

    6 egg yolks

    1 cup sugar

    2 cups heavy cream

⊙ Put the milk in a small saucepan with the cinnamon over medium heat, stirring until well combined. Cook, stirring now and then, until the milk is steaming hot but not quite boiling.

⊙ While the milk is heating, put the egg yolks in a large mixing bowl with the sugar and beat until the mixture is light and fluffy. Stir about one-third of the hot milk into the egg yolk mixture, then transfer the mixture to the saucepan and cook, stirring, until the mixture is once again steaming hot but not quite boiling. Take the custard off the heat and transfer it to the bowl used for the egg yolks.

⊙ Chill the custard completely, then stir in the cream and freeze in an ice cream maker according to the manufacturer's instructions. Transfer the ice cream to an airtight container and store it in the freezer until serving time.

Where *a* Turkey Meets *the* Sea

A Thanksgiving Dinner

MOIST *and* TENDER TURKEY *with* MADEIRA PAN GRAVY

CORNBREAD *and* OYSTER DRESSING

CRANBERRY-ORANGE RELISH

WHIPPED YUKON GOLD POTATOES

GINGERED GREEN BEANS

KABOCHA PUMPKIN TART

FOUR-NUT TART

The ice chest was at the bottom of the basement stairs, and an innocent visitor would never have guessed what was inside. But I knew, and my wife, Betsy, knew, that under the reinforced plastic lid of that innocuous-looking Coleman cooler, a body was bobbing around in salt water. Granted, the body was that of a turkey, but that was weird enough.

"It's like a scene from a Hitchcock movie," said Betsy. "I just can't stop thinking about it." When a friend came by, dropping off one of our children after a play date, and looked sideways at the cooler, we wanted to shout, "Do you realize there's a body in that cooler?!"

"We're brining our turkey," we told her instead. "Do you want to see it?" And when we lifted the lid of the cooler, you could almost hear the soundtrack from *Psycho.*

"Oh my God!" said our friend. "It's so weird."

The weird factor alone would motivate me to brine a turkey again, but what initially put me on the salty road to soaking a bird in seasoned water was the possibility of getting more moisture and flavor out of the biggest meal of the year. The ancient art of brining, or salting, was originally used to preserve meats intended for storage, but the technique has been carried on in the age of refrigeration because the process gives meat, especially poultry, a better texture and a satisfying—albeit somewhat salty—flavor.

It might seem that salt would actually dry meat out, but, because of a phenomenon known as Brownian motion, a salt-water bath actually renders meat more moist. English botanist Robert Brown noticed in 1827 that particles suspended in liquid tend to move about willy-nilly in every direction, even if the water is still. Chemists later determined that this random motion results in a more or less even distribution of particles. For a turkey, that means an exchange of particles is taking place between the turkey and its bathwater. The bird soaks up some saltwater and actually gains a little water weight, so the resulting roast is indeed juicier. The brine is later discarded, so even though the turkey does take up some salt, the vast majority of it is thrown out with the bathwater.

When I published a recipe for a brined turkey in the *Seattle Times* it generated a lot of response. Dozens of people told me it was the best turkey they had ever eaten. My family and I used the recipe before, during, and after its publication in the paper and thought it was great. (Admittedly, we like salty food.) But several other readers informed me in no uncertain terms that I had ruined their Thanksgiving by giving them a recipe for a salty disaster. It seems that some birds absorbed a lot more salt than others. I apologized profusely and questioned the complainers closely about what they did that might have yielded saltier results than mine. One reader, it seemed, neglected to add the ice water called for in the recipe, and another used denser table salt instead of kosher salt, but most apparently followed the recipe to the letter and still ended up with oversalted turkey. The problems, I concluded, are most likely to arise with prebasted turkeys and those that have been previously frozen. Since then, to be on the safe side, I have cut the amount of salt in the recipe in half. It still benefits from added moisture and flavor, but no longer threatens with too much salt.

A big challenge for the home cook is finding enough cold space to brine the bird. Even in the best of times, the average home refrigerator barely has room for a turkey, let alone a turkey in a tub. My fridge, for example, is almost always full of condiments that leave hardly any shelf space for real food. Hence the ice chest. It gets the bird out of the fridge altogether and allows more room for things like chutney and extra cranberry sauce, so essential for making good sandwiches once the whole turkey is rendered into leftovers.

It's very important that the turkey stay cold during the brining process. Otherwise bacteria will have an opportunity to spoil the meat. Make sure the brine is cold when it goes on the turkey, and use gel ice packs to keep it cold while the bird is soaking. (Likewise, leftover turkey needs to be refrigerated immediately after dinner.)

The Day Before

A great deal of the work involved in making a Thanksgiving dinner can be done ahead. The turkey, of course, has to be roasted on the day of the feast, but some of the messy work will be out of the way once it's put to soak in its bath of brine. Prepare the ingredients for the stuffing—bake the cornbread, cut the vegetables—but don't combine them until just before you bake them. Prepare the relish days ahead if you like, and store it in a tightly sealed jar in the refrigerator; it will only improve in flavor as it ages. The butter pastry for the tart crusts can be made ahead, rolled out, and kept frozen in the tart pans, ready to fill.

On the Table

In our family, it is a tradition for one of the kids to make place cards for everyone at the dinner. Over the years, we have had everything from pinecone-turkey place card holders and peculiar-looking construction paper objects to some really elegant cards with our names in calligraphy. The centerpieces have been a mixed bag too. A particularly hideous cornucopia of dried flowers made its rounds as a white elephant gift before it finally retired to my basement one year. But we've also seen some beautiful arrangements of end-of-the-season roses and grapes on their vines. It's a family holiday where virtually anything goes.

What to Pour

Since the best Thanksgiving dinners usually involve underage family members, something nonalcoholic is mandatory; in my family, we pour a combination of cranberry juice and ginger ale for the kids. And while people sometimes fret over what sort of wine to pour with turkey, it's been my experience that just about any wine works. Among the middle

150

generation, reds are generally preferred, and these have ranged from the most elegant pinot noirs to the heartiest zinfandels. The older generation likes white wine with their bird, and lively Alsatian Rieslings have proven especially popular.

Make It Simpler

This is an all-out gangbuster of a menu, but there's no reason that some of the tasks can't be farmed out to other members of the clan. If it seems too overwhelming, skip the tarts and let someone else bring the pie, focus on the main dish, and ask for help with the vegetables.

MOIST *and* TENDER TURKEY *with* MADEIRA PAN GRAVY

While the brine in which this turkey gets prepared for the oven isn't exactly ocean water, it does bear a certain relationship to Homer's wine-dark sea. The pre-soak enhances both the turkey's texture and its flavor. Be sure to use kosher salt, or if kosher salt is not available, use only half as much table salt.

SERVES 12 WITH LEFTOVERS

1 naturally raised turkey, about 16 pounds

1 gallon hot tap water

2 cups kosher salt

2 cups brown sugar

2 tablespoons whole black peppercorns

4 bay leaves

1 gallon ice water

6 cups water

1 carrot, sliced

1 medium onion, sliced

2 stalks celery, sliced

Madeira Pan Gravy (recipe follows)

⊙ The night before you plan to serve the turkey, wash out a 3-gallon cooler or container just large enough to hold the bird. Unwrap the turkey. Remove the giblets and refrigerate. Put the turkey in the clean cooler.

⊙ To make the brine, pour the gallon of hot tap water into a 3-gallon stockpot and bring it to a boil. Stir the salt, brown sugar, peppercorns, and bay leaves into the boiling water, turn off the heat, and let the mixture steep for 20 minutes. Stir in the ice water and continue stirring until the ice has melted.

⊙ Pour the cold brine over the turkey in the cooler or container; cover the cooler or put the container in the refrigerator. Allow the turkey to soak in the cold brine for 12 to 24 hours. Use gel ice packs if necessary to keep the brine cold.

⊙ Preheat the oven to 325°F. Transfer the turkey from the cooler to a roasting pan and discard the brine. Roast the turkey until the thigh meat registers 180°F, about 3¾ to 4¼ hours, or 15 minutes per pound. During the last hour of roasting, you may need to loosely cover the bird with aluminum foil to prevent overbrowning.

⊙ Meanwhile, bring the giblets to a boil in a large saucepan with the 6 cups water, carrot, onion, and celery, reduce heat to low, and simmer for 2 to 3 hours; add more water if needed to keep the giblets covered. Strain the turkey broth and set it aside, to use for making the gravy. You should end up with about 4 cups of broth.

⊙ Transfer the turkey to a platter, setting aside the roasting pan to use for making the gravy. Let the turkey rest for 20 minutes before carving. Serve it hot with the gravy.

Madeira Pan Gravy

Before it was brought to the table or even the cellar, Madeira used to be stored in the holds of merchant ships that sailed through the tropics. The time at sea aged and darkened this unique fortified wine, which has a long history with American food dating back to colonial times. Here it provides a perfect flavor bridge between the cornbread and oyster stuffing and the brined turkey.

MAKES ABOUT 4 CUPS

    I cup Madeira or sherry

    Reserved turkey broth, made from the giblets

    3 tablespoons cornstarch

    3 tablespoons water

⊙ Pour the Madeira into the roasting pan used for the turkey, and swirl it around to free up any flavorful bits of turkey clinging to the pan.

⊙ Add the reserved broth made from the giblets. Transfer the mixture to a medium saucepan and bring it to a full, rolling boil over high heat. In a small mixing bowl, dissolve the cornstarch in the water and whisk the mixture into the boiling broth. Boil it for 1 minute, then transfer to a gravy boat and serve hot.

CORNBREAD *and* OYSTER DRESSING

Sweet cornbread and salty oysters make this dressing extra flavorful. The lightest dressing is made with bread that was baked a day in advance and allowed to dry out. In a pinch, the cornbread can be cut into bits and toasted in a hot oven until it dries out a little. Since the brined turkey might make the dressing overly salty, bake the "stuffing" in a separate baking dish.

MAKES ABOUT 12 CUPS

6 tablespoons (3/4 stick) butter

1 medium onion, cut into 1/4-inch dice

4 stalks celery, cut into 1/4-inch dice

3 carrots, cut into 1/4-inch dice

2 dozen medium oysters, shucked, with their liquor

3 eggs

2 tablespoons chopped fresh sage, or 2 teaspoons dried

2 teaspoons kosher salt

2 teaspoons freshly ground black pepper

1 teaspoon ground nutmeg

12 cups day-old Cornbread, cut into 1-inch cubes (recipe follows)

⊙ Preheat the oven to 350°F and butter a 9- by 13-inch baking dish.

⊙ Melt the butter in a large sauté pan over medium-high heat. Add the onion, celery, and carrots and cook, stirring occasionally, until they are soft and beginning to brown, about 10 minutes. Add the oysters and sauté just until they firm up and curl around the edges, about 3 minutes. Take the sauté pan off the heat and allow the contents to cool completely.

155

⊙ In a very large mixing bowl, beat the eggs with the sage, salt, pepper, and nutmeg. Stir in the sautéed vegetables and oysters. Gently fold in the cornbread, being careful to keep it in chunks and not reduce it to crumbs.

⊙ Transfer the stuffing to the buttered baking dish, cover it with baker's parchment and then aluminum foil, and bake for 30 minutes. Remove the parchment and foil and bake for 10 minutes longer. Serve hot.

Cornbread

This recipe for cornbread is a double-batch version of the recipe I use quite often for simple family suppers. If no jelly-roll pan is available, use a 9- by 13-inch baking dish or a pair of 9-inch round cake pans, and lengthen the baking time to 20 or 25 minutes.

MAKES ENOUGH FOR 18 CUPS OF CUBES
- 2 cups flour
- 2 cups cornmeal
- 2 tablespoons baking powder
- 2 teaspoons salt
- 2 eggs
- 1 cup brown sugar
- 1 cup corn oil
- 2 cups milk

⊙ Preheat the oven to 400°F and butter an 11- by 17-inch jelly-roll pan.

⊙ In a large mixing bowl, whisk together the flour, cornmeal, baking powder, and salt.

◉ In the bowl of an electric mixer or in a medium mixing bowl with a whisk, beat the eggs, then beat in the brown sugar and corn oil. When these are thoroughly combined, beat in the milk.

◉ Add the egg mixture all at once to the dry ingredients, stirring just until well combined; do not overmix.

◉ Transfer the batter to the buttered pan and bake for 15 minutes, or until golden brown. Cut into 24 squares and serve hot.

CRANBERRY-ORANGE RELISH

Cranberries, grown in bogs near the ocean, are almost mandatory with turkey. With the bright, fresh addition of orange, this relish is irresistible.

MAKES ABOUT 3 CUPS

12 ounces ($^3/_4$ pound) fresh cranberries

Zest and juice from 1 medium orange

$^1/_2$ cup sugar

⊙ Put the cranberries in a medium nonreactive (stainless steel or enamel) saucepan over medium-high heat with the orange zest, orange juice, and sugar. Cook, stirring, until the sugar is dissolved and the mixture is beginning to boil.

⊙ Cover, reduce heat to low, and cook until the cranberries have burst, 8 to 10 minutes.

⊙ The relish may be served at once or kept, covered and refrigerated, for several days.

WHIPPED YUKON GOLD POTATOES

Yukon Gold, German Butterball, and Yellow Finn potatoes are yellow-fleshed, smooth-textured, and thin-skinned varieties that are excellent for mashing. If the potatoes are cut in uniform small dice, they will cook evenly. Cut this way, they need not be peeled.

MAKES ABOUT 12 CUPS
>   5 pounds Yukon Gold potatoes
>   1 tablespoon kosher salt
>   1/4 cup canola oil

⊙ Scrub the potatoes thoroughly and cut them into 1-inch dice. Put the diced potatoes and salt in a heavy, 1-gallon stockpot, and add water to barely cover. Bring to a boil over high heat, reduce heat to low and cook the potatoes until they are quite tender and beginning to fall apart, about 15 minutes.

⊙ Drain the potatoes in a colander, but save the cooking liquid. Put the drained potatoes back in the stockpot and whisk in the canola oil, mashing the potatoes in the process.

⊙ Whisk in just enough of the reserved cooking liquid to render the mashed potatoes smooth and creamy. Serve the potatoes at once, or keep them covered over the lowest possible heat for up to 20 minutes. Serve hot.

GINGERED GREEN BEANS

Boiled first in salted water then finished in a sauté pan with ginger, sugar, and salt, the green beans remain bright green, slightly crisp, and very flavorful.

SERVES 12

- 1 gallon water
- 2 tablespoons salt
- 2 pounds fresh green beans
- 1/4 cup canola oil
- 2 tablespoons grated fresh ginger
- 2 teaspoons sugar
- 2 teaspoons kosher salt

⊙ In a large 6-quart saucepan, bring the water to a boil and add the salt. Meanwhile, trim the stem ends from the green beans, leaving the tapered "tails" intact. Add the trimmed beans to the boiling water, and cook for 5 minutes. (The beans should remain bright green and be tender with a slight crunch.) Drain the beans and scatter them over a baking sheet to cool slightly and halt the cooking process. (The beans may be prepared up to this point a couple of hours in advance and finished just before serving.)

⊙ Put the canola oil in a large sauté pan, and add the ginger. (If you have a microplane grater, the easiest way is to grate the ginger directly into the pan.) Over high heat, sauté the ginger until it is sizzling, about 1 minute.

⊙ Add the parboiled green beans to the sauté pan, and sprinkle on the sugar and salt. Cook until the beans are heated through and perfumed with the ginger, about 2 to 3 minutes. Serve at once.

KABOCHA PUMPKIN TART

Thinner and somewhat more interesting than a traditional pumpkin pie, this tart is made with kabocha, the green-skinned Japanese pumpkin, which has a dense, meaty flesh far more flavorful than even the best pie pumpkins. Peeled, seeded, and diced, the squash cooks quickly in an old-fashioned steamer basket. If fresh squash is too hard to deal with, don't resort to a can, look for frozen squash. It's pretty widely available and infinitely better than canned pumpkin.

MAKES ONE 12-INCH TART

Butter Pastry Pie Crust (recipe follows)
1 medium kabocha squash, about 2 pounds
1 cup water
3 eggs
3/4 cup brown sugar
1 teaspoon ground cinnamon
1 teaspoon ground ginger
1/2 teaspoon ground allspice
1/2 teaspoon kosher salt
1/2 cup heavy cream
Whipped cream or Cinnamon Ice Cream (page 145)

⊙ Make the butter pastry and place it in a two-piece 12-inch tart pan.

⊙ Cut the squash into wedges, scrape out the seeds, then cut away the peel. Cut the peeled and seeded squash into 1-inch dice. You should have about 5 cups of diced squash.

161

⊙ Pile the diced squash into a steamer basket. Put the steamer basket in a heavy, 1-gallon stockpot and add the water. Steam the squash over high heat until tender, about 10 minutes. Put the steamed squash in a food processor and purée until smooth. You should have about 2½ cups of purée. (Note: The squash purée may be made in advance and kept refrigerated for a day or two before making the pie.)

⊙ Preheat the oven to 350°F.

⊙ Whisk the puréed steamed squash in a large mixing bowl with the eggs, brown sugar, cinnamon, ginger, allspice, salt, and cream. Pour the squash filling into the tart pan and bake until the filling is puffed and its edges are beginning to crack, about 40 minutes. Cool the pie slightly before removing the sides of the tart pan. Use a long metal spatula to free the bottom crust from the pan and transfer the tart to a serving plate. Serve warm or at room temperature with scoops of cinnamon ice cream or dollops of fresh whipped cream.

Butter Pastry *for* Tarts

A simple butter pastry is infinitely better than one full of shortening made from hydrogenated oil. Very often, if I'm making one tart, I'll make two crusts and freeze one for the future.

MAKES I CRUST

1 cup all-purpose flour
½ cup (1 stick) cold unsalted butter, cut into ½-inch bits
½ teaspoon salt
3 tablespoons cold water

⊙ In a food processor, combine the flour, butter, and salt. Process just until the mixture resembles coarse crumbs; leave some chunks of butter about the size of small peas. (If no food processor is available, combine the flour and salt in a mixing bowl and cut in the butter with a pastry cutter, a fork, or your fingers.)

⊙ Transfer the flour-and-butter mixture to a large mixing bowl and sprinkle the cold water on top. Work the water into the flour mixture just until the dough comes together into a scrappy mass. Do not knead or overwork; it is not necessary to make the dough into a smooth ball. Roll the dough into a circle and place the circle in a two-piece tart pan (for the recipes above) or a pie pan. Trim the edges of the dough and bake or fill as instructed in the recipe. (Note: The pastry may be made several days in advance and kept frozen until just before filling and baking.)

FOUR-NUT TART

The nuts in this tart should be spread out in a single layer, so a shallow, 12-inch tart pan works much better than a deep-dish 9- or 10-inch pie pan. If a shallow tart pan is not available, consider baking the tart in a rectangular 9- by 13-inch cake pan to make it thinner.

MAKES ONE 12-INCH TART

Butter Pastry (page 162)
1 cup pecans
1 cup walnuts
1 cup macadamia nuts
1/2 cup pine nuts
3 eggs
1 cup sugar
1 cup dark corn syrup
2 tablespoons walnut oil
1 teaspoon vanilla extract
1/2 teaspoon salt
Heavy cream, whipped, as an accompaniment

⊙ Make the butter pastry and place it in a two-piece 12-inch tart pan.

⊙ Preheat the oven to 350°F. Spread the four different nuts onto the unbaked pie crust in the tart pan, distributing them as evenly as you can.

⊙ Whisk together the eggs and sugar in a mixing bowl. Stir in the corn syrup, walnut oil, vanilla extract, and salt. Pour this mixture over the nuts.

◉ Bake the tart until the filling is browned and beginning to puff up, about 45 minutes. Cool for 30 minutes before serving.

◉ Remove the sides of the tart pan. Use a long metal spatula to free the bottom crust from the pan and transfer the tart to a serving plate. Serve at room temperature with dollops of fresh whipped cream.

Observing *the* Winter Solstice
A Holiday Supper *for* Extended Family

||||||||||||||||||||||||||||||||||||||||||||||||||||||||||||||||||||||||||||||||||||||||||||||||||||||||||||||||||||||||||||||||||||||||||||||||||||

FAVORITE BREAD ROLLS

OYSTER BISQUE

WINTER GREENS SALAD *with* SWEET ORANGE VINAIGRETTE

TWICE-ROASTED DUCKLING *with* BRANDY *and*
    CRACKED PEPPER SAUCE

BRAISED CHESTNUTS *and* BRUSSELS SPROUTS

YULE LOG CAKE

Like so many other people who live in and around Seattle, I came here from somewhere else. And while I love it here and have been here longer than I have ever been anywhere else, I can't help but feel nostalgic about the places I left behind, the life I might have lived had I stayed closer to my roots. Newcomers, immigrants, settlers from abroad miss not so much the places they came from as the traditions. And for me, the traditions I miss were barely formed. My parents and my grandparents before them were always embracing new ways of doing things, so traditions had a hard time taking root. Now, as a transplant living far away from my childhood home, I sometimes feel that I am forever reinventing myself and my family, while, ironically, searching for some consistent thread in our routine.

And for me, the winter solstice marks an opportunity to connect old and new. Some parts of the country are always snowy at Christmas, while other places stay pretty warm, but here we could go either way. The light is rhythmic, though. In summer the days are long, almost too long, and in winter they are short and dark. I am always strangely elated when the days grow short and the nights grow long and the magical time of the winter solstice approaches. A nip in the air and a sky full of clouds promise—but usually fail to deliver—a blanket of snow, and we start thinking about Christmas or, more precisely, Christmas dinner. Every year I dream up a new menu. One year it's my grandfather's ham or a grand roast beef, the next year it's a Dickensian goose.

Try as we might to establish traditions, Christmas at our house is a little different every year. I hope that, seen through the mists of time, some pattern will emerge in the memories of our children. But I can't imagine what it will be. Some years we go to Betsy's sister's house and have Christmas there. Other years we settle into a vacation home lent to us by some family friends. Still other years, we travel.

If anything remains consistent, it is the Christmas tree. Every year we purchase a tree from the local Boy Scout troop and drag it into the living room, to be dressed in the traditional assortment of lights and ornaments brought up from the basement. I do the lights, and Betsy and the boys do the rest. I like to imagine that I am calm and competent with the lights, but the rest of my family says I get tense and snappy when I'm crawling around under the tree, wrapping the branches with electrical cords. They often make themselves scarce. "Hey, where did everybody go?" I call out from the corner behind the tree. "I need someone to pass me this cord!"

"See," they whisper to one another from the next room, "he's getting testy now."

I think the people who lived in our house before us bought live Christmas trees, small ones that didn't take up as much room in the house as the large cut trees we haul in every year. The house is roughly a hundred years old, and the couple who lived here immediately before us occupied the place for thirty years. They were serious gardeners and avid collectors of things. When we moved in, the basement was full of hardware, scraps of wood, flowerpots, and magazines. So for a long time after we moved in, we felt we were living in their house. When we gardened, we were like caretakers, tending of their plants. When we cleaned the basement, we were timid about disturbing too many of their things. Call us crazy, but that's how we are.

Both Betsy and I are the youngest children in our large families, and we both have a tremendous capacity to accept things as they are. Okay, I'll wear these red corduroy pants that don't quite fit. Sure, I'll eat the wing of the turkey if that's the piece you don't want. Yes, you can leave those thirty-five paint cans in the basement; maybe we'll use them someday.

Only after a period of years have we come to realize that the house and the garden are really ours, and we can get rid of things we don't like. After a year or so of complaining about them, we tore out the ugly bathroom fixtures and replaced them. And gradually, we have replaced some of the couple's garden plants with plants we like better. For as long as we could, we carefully tended their two fifty-foot rows of bearded iris, but then one year we pulled out all the iris bulbs and replaced them with herbs and roses and peonies.

One change we were especially slow to make was the removal of some of the various coniferous trees that were planted all around the place. These, I believe, were the previous family's Christmas trees. They seemed to be invested with a lot of good feelings, and it seemed cold and indifferent to rip them out. But they were planted too close together, and they were crowding out some trees we liked better: volunteer fig trees, a sweet Lady apple tree, and two wonderful gingkos. So finally, we invited a friend with a chain saw to come over and dispense with the old overgrown Christmas trees.

One of the old trees, though, was too beautiful, too well situated, and too well established to remove. It's a mature noble fir and, standing as it does in front of an old boxwood hedge, it really lives up to its name. It is taller than the house and exudes a gracious combination of grandeur and humility that only trees in their prime can muster. It has personality.

After we had been in the house for a few years and had begun to establish our own customs here, it occurred to me to dress the old noble fir with Christmas lights. We talked about using simple white lights because they seemed more tasteful, but in the end we went for color. I bought a half-dozen strands of big-bulbed, old-fashioned, multicolored outdoor lights, and a glowing white star for the top.

Then, even though it was raining and the wind was blowing what felt like twenty knots and the thermometer was dipping into the low forties, I put an aluminum paint ladder against the tree and climbed to the top. The ladder swayed along with the tree in the winter wind. My hands grew numb and the rain-drenched branches whipped against my legs until I was soaked to the skin. But I was strangely excited by all this, undeterred. The tree was larger than I realized, so the lights I bought were not enough. I had to return to the store and buy more. And when we plugged them in, the fuses blew and the whole place went momentarily dark. We had to jury-rig a series of extension cords from different outlets to make the various strands of lights work together. Finally, though, the tree blazed merrily in the face of the cold gray winter weather.

That night, the rain turned quite unexpectedly to snow. In the morning, we turned on the lights on the outdoor Christmas tree, and from behind the billowing piles of snow on every branch, the big, colorful lights blazed in all their garish glory. It seemed almost as if the lights had summoned the snow. We skied and sledded and drank hot chocolate, and even though this was a one-time thing, it felt like something we had always done, something we would do again and again, year after year.

When the boys are grown and have children of their own, I hope they will all come to see us at Christmastime. And on the way, I hope they will tell their kids that every year when they were growing up, their dad would decorate the big noble fir in front of the house with colored lights, and snow would fall.

Nothing is the same every year at the dinner table, of course, but even though I tweak the Christmas menu all the time, some things do bear repeating. My brother-in-law loves duck and I love to cook duck, so whenever Christmas dinner is slated to occur at his house, I do duck. I like oyster bisque too, so even if we don't make it part of every Christmas dinner, I make sure that the dish appears at least once during the holiday season. And while my efforts to find the ultimate traditional Christmas dessert have led me to try trifle and toy with fruitcake, I keep coming back to the mocha-flavored Yule log cake.

I believe that if I were capable of doing anything the same way year after year, I would light up the noble fir outside and prepare this menu.

What to Pour

With oyster bisque, flavored as it is with sherry, more of the same would seem only natural, but trying to direct what anyone will drink at a Christmas dinner, especially during that critical hour before the meal, is futile. Let them have their chardonnay, their sparkling apple cider, whatever it is they like, but do hold back a couple of bottles of your best red wine until after the salad is cleared. When the duck comes to the table, pour a Washington-grown Syrah, a fine old Châteauneuf-du-Pape, or some other bold Rhône-style wine. Make it last until the Yule log cake is served with coffee.

On the Table

This is the big one, the feast to end all winter feasts, so break out your best clothes, linen napkins, fine china, crystal goblets, the works.

The Days Before

Most of the items in this menu can and should be made a day or two before. In mid-December, before things get too hectic, I make two Yule log cakes and keep them frozen until they are called for; they freeze and thaw beautifully. One is for Christmas dinner and the other is for the inevitable holiday potluck. The honey-roasted almonds can be made several days in advance; the only danger is that they will disappear before the day of the dinner. The duck should be roasted and boned a day or two before it is served to allow ample time for stock and sauce making. The vinaigrette can be made ahead, too.

Make It Simpler

The homemade rolls can be replaced with store-bought ones or forgone altogether. If someone in your clan is good at shucking them, oysters on the half shell might be easier—and, in some circles, more welcome—than the oyster bisque. If roast duck seems like too much, consider a simpler dish with some of the same flavors: Boneless breasts of duckling, available by special order from a good butcher or via the Internet, are much simpler to prepare. Simply pan-sear the breasts skin side down, then move them to a 400°F oven until they are crisp on top and barely cooked through, and an instant-read thermometer inserted in the center of a breast registers 145°F, about 10 minutes. A reasonable facsimile of the sauce can be made with chicken broth in place of the concentrated duck stock.

FAVORITE BREAD ROLLS

The recipe for these rolls has evolved over the years. My friend and cookbook author Terry Thompson taught me to add a little vinegar to my bread dough to give it more character.

MAKES 18 LARGE ROLLS

2 cups warm water

2 packages active dry yeast

2 tablespoons sugar

5 cups flour

2 tablespoons rice wine vinegar or other wine vinegar

2 tablespoons salt

⊙ In a large mixing bowl, stir together warm water, yeast, and sugar. Add flour, vinegar, and salt. Mix for 5 minutes or until smooth and elastic.

⊙ Allow dough to rise for 1 hour, or until doubled in size. Preheat the oven to 400°F and line two baking sheets with baker's parchment. On a floured work surface, divide dough into two strips about 4 inches wide, and cut each strip on the bias into 9 pieces. Turn each piece gently to taper the ends and form rolls.

⊙ Place 9 rolls on each lined baking sheet. Let rolls stand for 10 minutes at room temperature, then bake for 12 to 15 minutes, or until brown and crisp. Serve hot. The rolls may be baked ahead and reheated just before serving.

OYSTER BISQUE

It defies logic that a viscous gray soup could be so appetizing. But the myste-
rious mineral-toned flavor and the creamy-meaty texture make this soup one of
our all time favorites. On some winter nights, it's supper in itself.

SERVES 6 TO 8

2 cups water

4 dozen small, live oysters

1/4 cup (1/2 stick) butter

4 shallots, chopped

1/2 teaspoon freshly ground black pepper

About 1/8 teaspoon freshly grated nutmeg, or to taste

1/2 cup sherry or Madeira

3 cups heavy cream, divided

2 tablespoons chopped parsley for garnish

⊙ Bring the water to a boil. Scrub the oysters, add them to the water, and steam them until they open, about 10 minutes. Remove the oysters with a slotted spoon. Reserve the water.

⊙ Pull the steamed oysters out of their shells and put them in a blender. Carefully pour in most of the reserved steaming water; pour slowly, so that any grit or bits of shell sink into the pot and don't go into the blender. Discard the last bit of liquid. Blend the oysters and their liquor to make a fairly smooth purée.

⊙ Put the butter in a heavy, 1-gallon soup pot or Dutch oven over medium-high heat and add the shallots. Sauté until they are soft and transparent, about 2 minutes. Add the pepper, nutmeg, and sherry; cook until the sherry has evaporated and the shallots have begun to sizzle in the pan once again, about 5 minutes. Add 2½ cups of the cream and bring the mixture to a full, rolling boil; stir to prevent the cream from boiling over.

⊙ Whip the remaining cream and set aside. Stir the oyster purée into the boiling cream mixture. As soon as the oyster purée is heated through, about 1 minute, serve the soup hot with the cream and chopped parsley on top.

WINTER GREENS SALAD *with* SWEET ORANGE VINAIGRETTE

The flavors of oranges and almonds bring winter greens to life. The same combination works well with spinach.

SERVES 6

I pound prewashed, mixed organic salad greens

½ cup Sweet Orange Vinaigrette (recipe follows)

I cup Honey-Roasted Almonds (recipe follows)

⊙ Toss the salad greens with the vinaigrette and distribute evenly between serving plates. Scatter the honey-roasted almonds over each salad and serve at once.

Sweet Orange Vinaigrette

For years, I've used the reduced (concentrated) juices of citrus fruits in place of vinegar in salad dressings. I would boil down the fresh juice and replace the water that boiled away with oil to make a smooth and zesty dressing. In a pinch one day, I reached for frozen orange juice concentrate and found that it made a beautiful dressing. White balsamic vinegar adds extra zing. Serve it with any mixed green salad.

MAKES ABOUT 2 CUPS

I can (6 ounces) frozen organic orange juice concentrate

¼ cup white balsamic vinegar or lemon juice

I tablespoon sugar

1½ teaspoons kosher salt

½ teaspoon ground white pepper

I cup canola oil

177

◉ Put the orange juice concentrate in a blender with the balsamic vinegar, sugar, salt, and white pepper, and blend until they are well combined. With the blender running, slowly stream in the canola oil to create a smooth emulsion. The vinaigrette will keep, covered and refrigerated, for several weeks.

Honey-Roasted Almonds

A three-step process flavors these crispy almonds intensely. Toast the nuts alone; toss them in a hot mixture of honey, oil, and almond syrup (I use the kind seen at espresso stands); and then finish them in a coating of sugar and salt. The variations are limitless: other nuts, other flavors of syrup, the addition of spices to the finishing coat of sugar. During the holiday party season, a tin of these makes a great hostess gift.

MAKES 4 CUPS

4 cups almonds

Coating Mix

1/4 cup sugar
1 tablespoon kosher salt

Glaze

1 tablespoon honey
1 tablespoon almond oil or butter
1 tablespoon almond-flavored syrup

⊙ Preheat the oven to 350°F.

⊙ Toast the almonds in the oven until they take on a warm toasted smell and turn golden brown in color, about 10 minutes. Meanwhile, put the sugar and salt in a large mixing bowl and set aside.

⊙ In a large frying pan over high heat, combine the honey, almond oil, and almond-flavored syrup, and stir until the mixture is boiling. Stir the hot toasted almonds into the boiling glaze and cook, stirring or tossing, for 1 to 2 minutes, or until the glaze is dried up.

⊙ Toss the hot, glazed nuts in the bowl of sugar and salt to coat, then scatter them over a baking sheet or a tray in a single layer. Cool completely before storing in an airtight container.

TWICE-ROASTED DUCKLING *with* BRANDY *and* CRACKED PEPPER SAUCE

While the following recipe may appear difficult, most capable cooks with decent kitchen equipment will find it quite manageable. The process is time consuming, but it doesn't require any special knowledge or skill. If you divide the preparation over a span of two days, with less than an hour actually devoted to tending the duck, the process won't leave you frazzled, and the results will be well worth the time involved. Roast and bone the duck the day before you plan to serve it, and make the stock from the bones and giblets. Then, the next day, make the sauce from the stock and crisp the boned duckling in a hot oven just before you plan to serve it. If you plan to shorten the menu and make the duckling the whole show, then serve each person half a duckling; if you serve all the courses in this menu, one quarter-duckling per person is ample.

MAKES 4 LARGE PORTIONS OR 8 SMALLER ONES
2 whole ducklings with giblets
Kosher salt and freshly ground black pepper, to taste
1 onion, sliced but not peeled
1 carrot, chopped
1 stalk celery, chopped
2 bay leaves
3 whole cloves
8 cups water
Brandy and Cracked Pepper Sauce (recipe follows)

Roasting

⊙ Preheat the oven to 400°F. Remove the giblets from the ducks and discard the livers; reserve the remaining giblets, and refrigerate while the ducks are roasting. Sprinkle the ducks generously inside and out with salt and pepper.

⊙ Put the seasoned ducks in a large roasting pan at least 4 inches deep, and roast for 1 hour. Remove the birds from the oven and allow them to cool until they can be easily handled.

Boning

⊙ To split the ducks in half, place a bird, breast side up, on a stable cutting board with the legs pointing away from you. Using a sharp chef's knife, cut into the bottom of the breastplate and through the cartilage, all the way to the top. Spread the split carcass open to gain access to the spine. Placing the blade along one side of the backbone, press firmly and rock until the blade is all the way through. Place the blade along the other side of the spine and cut through. You should have two half-ducks and a spine. Repeat with the other duck.

⊙ Next, on each half-duck, run your thumb between the cartilage and the breast meat. With your thumb, carefully separate meat from bone along the ribcage toward the wing, and then, with a sharp twist, remove the ribcage. Remove the pelvic bones in the same manner.

⊙ The bones of the thighs and legs will remain. Trim the wings down to the first joint. Reserve the bones for the stock. Wrap and chill the boned duck-halves for several hours, while you make the stock, or overnight.

Making the stock

⊙ In a heavy 1-gallon stockpot, combine the reserved giblets, the bones, and the onion, carrot, celery, bay leaves, and cloves. Cover with the water and bring to a boil. Reduce heat and simmer gently for 4 hours or longer. Strain the liquid, discard the solids, and chill or set aside the stock for use in the brandy sauce.

Serving

⊙ Preheat oven to 400°F.

⊙ Remove the duck halves from the refrigerator, and cut them in half again if desired. Arrange them in a roasting pan and bake until crispy and well-browned, about 20 minutes.

⊙ Place each piece of duck on a serving plate and ladle on the brandy sauce.

Brandy *and* Cracked Pepper Sauce

Built on a base of caramelized sugar and cracked peppercorns, this sauce is rich and deeply flavored.

MAKES 1½ CUPS

2 tablespoons whole black peppercorns

2 tablespoons sugar

¼ cup brandy

1 cup heavy cream

1½ cups concentrated duck stock, made from duck bones

⊙ Crack the peppercorns by using the blunt side of a chef's knife to crush them against a cutting board. (Or put them in a clean coffee grinder reserved for grinding pepper, and pulse the grinder on and off until the peppercorns are broken into bits but not finely ground.)

⊙ In a large saucepan, melt the sugar over high heat by swirling the pan around. Add the peppercorns and the brandy and step back; the melted sugar will harden on contact with the liquid. If the burner is an open flame, the brandy may ignite. Boil and burn to eliminate most of the alcohol, about 1 minute.

⊙ Add the cream and stir until the caramelized sugar has all remelted; boil until it is reduced to half of its original volume. Add the concentrated duck stock and cook, stirring, until the sauce is slightly thickened, about 5 minutes.

BRAISED CHESTNUTS *and* BRUSSELS SPROUTS

Pairing chestnuts and Brussels sprouts is a tradition in Europe. The slightly bitter sprouts are tempered by the sweet nuts. If fresh chestnuts are unavailable or if they seem like too much trouble, chestnuts canned in water may be substituted.

SERVES 6

1 pound fresh chestnuts, about 36

1 pound Brussels sprouts

2 quarts water

2 tablespoons salt

1 cup chicken broth

⊙ Put a large pot of water on to boil the chestnuts. With a sharp paring knife, cut a cross in the shell of each chestnut. Try not to cut down into the meat of the nut, but do cut through the shell so the nuts will be easy to peel when they are roasted. Boil the cut chestnuts for 5 minutes. Scoop them out of the water with a strainer or slotted spoon.

⊙ While the chestnuts are still hot, pull off the outer shells and peel off as much of the inner skin as you can. If some of the nuts will not give up their skins, reheat them and try again; if necessary, cut away any stubborn bits of skin with a paring knife.

⊙ Use the paring knife to trim the bottoms from the Brussels sprouts. Pull away any loose or damaged leaves. Put the 2 quarts water and salt in a large saucepan, and bring to a boil. Add the Brussels sprouts and boil for 4 to 5 minutes, or until they can be easily pierced with the tip of a knife. Drain the sprouts and rinse in cold water to halt the cooking process.

⊙ Put the peeled chestnuts in a large sauté pan with the chicken broth and simmer gently for 5 minutes. Do not let the broth boil too hard or the chestnuts will fall apart. As soon as the chestnuts are tender, add the Brussels sprouts and cook uncovered for another 5 minutes. (If using canned chestnuts, cook the broth over high heat until it is reduced to about half its original volume before adding the chestnuts.)

⊙ If the sauce has not reduced into a syrupy glaze around the chestnuts and Brussels sprouts, lift the vegetables out with a slotted spoon. Boil the broth in the pan until it is almost gone, then return the vegetables to the pan and toss them in the reduced broth to coat them. Serve hot as a side dish.

YULE LOG CAKE

Even before Christmas was celebrated in Europe, people marked the winter solstice with feasting. On the darkest night of the year, a log was kept burning until dawn to prevent the light of the world from going out. Today, the tradition is maintained with a cake fashioned in the shape of a log.

SERVES 12

Chocolate Bark (recipe follows)
6 eggs, separated
1 cup sugar, divided
1 teaspoon salt
¹/₂ cup (1 stick) butter, melted and cooled
1 teaspoon vanilla extract
1 cup flour, divided
Coffee Buttercream (recipe follows)

⊙ Preheat the oven to 350°F. Butter an 11- by 17-inch jelly-roll pan and line it with baker's parchment.

⊙ Make the chocolate bark and, as directed in the recipe, spread it over baker's parchment and chill until set.

⊙ Meanwhile, in a large mixing bowl, combine the egg yolks with ½ cup of the sugar and beat until light. Stir in the salt, butter, and vanilla extract.

⊙ In a large dry mixing bowl, beat the egg whites until they hold soft peaks, then add the remaining sugar gradually, beating all the while.

⊙ Fold one-third of the egg white mixture and ½ cup flour into the yolk mixture, stirring just until lumps are gone. Fold in another third of the egg whites and the remainder of the flour. Fold in the remaining egg whites.

◉ Transfer the batter to the jelly-roll pan and bake for 20 minutes, or until the cake springs back when pressed lightly in the center.

◉ While the cake is still hot, roll it into a log shape, with the baker's parchment still attached. Allow the rolled-up cake to cool, then unroll it and peel off the parchment.

◉ Spread half of the buttercream over the cake and roll it back up. Spread the remaining buttercream over the surface.

◉ Remove the chocolate bark from the refrigerator. Wrap the chilled bark, with the parchment still attached, around the frosted cake and chill again. If the bark is too stiff, let it stand at room temperature until pliable, about 5 minutes. Once the cake is wrapped, carefully peel away the parchment. Cut one end off the cake and place it on the side of the cake to represent a sawed-off branch.

Chocolate Bark

2 cups (one 12-ounce bag) semisweet chocolate chips
1/4 cup canola oil

◉ Line a baking sheet with baker's parchment and set aside. Put the chocolate chips and canola oil in a small saucepan over medium-low heat, and stir until the chocolate is melted. Spread the melted chocolate over the parchment and chill until the chocolate is set.

Coffee Buttercream

While American confectioners' sugar–based icings have their place (consider the mocha frosting for Celia's Cakes on page 21), French-style buttercream is something utterly different. The emphasis is on the butter—not the sugar— and the texture is incomparably smooth. If the buttercream seems too runny, or if it breaks, the problem is one of temperature; simply cool it down or warm it up and whisk constantly until the desired smooth and fluffy texture is achieved.

MAKES ABOUT 2 CUPS

1 cup sugar

1/3 cup water

2 egg yolks

1 whole egg

1/2 teaspoon salt

1 1/2 cups (3 sticks) unsalted butter, at room temperature

2 tablespoons strong espresso or coffee

1 tablespoon dark rum

1 teaspoon vanilla extract

◉ Stir the sugar and water in a saucepan over medium-high heat until the sugar is dissolved. Then let the syrup cook undisturbed for 5 minutes, or until a bit of the syrup makes a soft ball when dropped into a cup of cold water. (A candy thermometer will register 235°F.)

⊙ Beat the egg yolks, the whole egg, and salt in the bowl of an electric mixer or in a large mixing bowl with a whisk, until light and fluffy. With the mixer running on medium speed, stream in the sugar syrup. Reduce the mixing speed to low and drop in the butter a little at a time. Add the espresso, rum, and vanilla extract and continue mixing until the buttercream is smooth and spreadable.

A Menu *for* Romance
Valentine's Day
Supper *for* Two

||||||||||||||||||||||||||||||||||||||||||||||||||||||||||||||||||||||||||||||||||||||||||

"MATISSE BREAD" *or* FOUGASSE

THREE SHELLFISH *with* THREE CITRUS FRUITS

PROVENÇAL CHICKEN *with* TOMATO *and* ORANGE

SAUTÉED KALE *with* GARLIC

CHOCOLATE MARQUIS *with* SAFFRON CREAM

According to the best gardeners I know, the Pacific Northwest is blessed with a Mediterranean climate. Sometimes this baffles me. The Mediterranean I have visited is a sunny place, where people bask in glorious amber light under blazing blue skies. There, lemons ripen against the ancient stone walls of hilltop villages, and orchards full of olive trees reach deep into the soil of lands where the story of Western civilization unfolds like a pageant in real time. It's not like that here.

Here, we shudder under dripping cedar boughs and wrap up in Cowichan sweaters to go out in boats or dig clams from the shoreline. And yet there are moments, such as when I pluck a fig fully ripened in the warmth of a Pacific Northwest summer and bring it in a waft of fresh green perfume to my mouth, that I see the connection. Rosemary that started out in a four-inch pot seems overnight to have become a bush that looks as if it could have grown up in the ruins of a Roman coliseum. The row of lavender in my garden looks for all the world like a piece of the countryside around Grasse in the south of France, plucked up in its entirety and put down quite intact. The walnut trees that shiver in our long, wet Novembers seem to remember the mistral that blows up from Africa and turns cold against the south coast of France.

And then there are those moments when I am transported by some association between the two places into a piece of time that seems to lie neither here nor there, but in a realm all its own. Certain blocks of time do not fall neatly behind us in an orderly row of days gone by. They do not fit into any sort of procession at all, and they move instead like items hanging from a mobile sculpture. Sometimes, when I am standing with both feet firmly planted on Northwest soil, I am thrown, as if through a wormhole in time, headlong into a certain corner of Provence, where Betsy and I spent a winter when Henry was three years old.

According to Betsy's diary, there were particular dates one winter when we drove around Provence, in Aix, in Arles, in Les Baux, bundling ourselves against the wind and feeding our boy kilo after kilo of tiny vibrant oranges ripened in the dazzling winter light of the Riviera. But according to my internal reckoning, those days are suspended outside of time.

We stayed in the home of a friend in a town called Vence, a place that stands with its back pressed against the medieval town wall. Inside the wall, a market was held twice a week. And at that market, we found fresh seafood, winter vegetables, and citrus fruits as vibrant as the Provençal light that glowed from within them. There were country chickens, goat cheeses, and a bread that the baker called Matisse, after the artist who had called this town home for a number of years. On picnics, we ate clusters of strong, seedy grapes and small wheels of goat cheese sandwiched between crusts of country bread.

During that time I worked in the kitchen of the great master of Provençal cooking, Roger Vergé, at his Moulin de Mougins, which was at that time studded with three Michelin stars—or, as the French prefer to call them, *macarons*. While I worked at the restaurant, Betsy and little Henry were left to fend for themselves, and fend they did, discovering little towns along the coast, seemingly abandoned for the off-season. They found playgrounds and merry-go-rounds; and while the weary toddler napped in his stroller, my wife walked beside castles and fountains and in and out of shops buying food for our humble late-night suppers and her lunches with our boy.

When my "stage," or brief apprenticeship, was over, there were a thousand places my wife wanted me to see, and a dozen roads she had not followed until I could come with her. On my first Sunday off, we headed for a road that wound into the hills from a tiny village between the towns of Vence and Grasse. On the way to the village we passed narrow gorges where the river tumbled over cliffs and young people climbed stairs carved from the native rock to secret places behind the waterfalls.

The village had two bridges—one of them alive, and one of them bombed out but carefully preserved as a kind of memorial to the resistance movement that left all too few monuments during World War II. We stopped in the village for sparkling water and read the commemorative plaque. Then we started up the road. We followed its two narrow lanes, which rose like a wisp of smoke from the valley to one lofty height after another, until we were surrounded by woods. Then out of the woods came a tiny old woman with a huge bundle of sticks. She was every old woman in every fairy tale we'd ever read, and when we had slowed almost to a stop to let her pass, I jumped out and asked if we could take a picture of her. She stopped, smiled, and said she couldn't hear me.

"Can we make a photograph?" I pronounced the French words carefully. "With the camera?" And the smile disappeared.

"*Ah, non, non!*" she cried, then turned away and disappeared into the forest without looking back. Sometimes, now, when I am walking through the woods here on Bainbridge Island, thousands of miles away, I imagine I can see the old woman with her bundle of sticks rounding the next bend in the trail.

When we came home to Washington, I immediately started trying to re-create some of the foods we grew to love during our few short months in the south of France. And soon, the techniques and the aesthetics I had almost unconsciously absorbed while I was there began to influence all sorts of things I cooked. Now certain foods carry me back to that place. I can hardly peel an orange without remembering the way they hung in clusters from the trees around the courtyards of Grasse. And whenever I squeeze a lemon, I smell not only its fragrance but the dust that rose dry and cold around the trees we saw in Menton, where a local legend claims that Eve first planted lemons when she snuck them out of the Garden of Eden.

And best of all, our son Erich, the ultimate souvenir, was conceived on a moonlit night in Vence during the winter that Betsy and I spent in the land of romance.

The Day Before

Bake the bread the day before and reheat it just before serving. The citrus fruits to garnish the shellfish may be prepared ahead of time but must be introduced to the seafood only a short time before they are served. The chicken can be made hours ahead and kept in a warm oven. The meat will begin to fall off the bones, rendering it more of a stew, but this should not be a problem.

What to Pour

A Provençal rosé is the wine I would choose, but a deep red Rhône would be equally apropos. A Washington rosé made from cabernet franc would also be an excellent choice.

On the Table

Candles are mandatory here, and if they are made of genuine beeswax, so much the better. Real silver and crockery with a deep green glaze will also help set the mood.

"MATISSE BREAD" *or* FOUGASSE

I discovered this style of bread in the small Provençal town called Vence. There, on market days, the baker sold it as Matisse bread because Matisse, who once lived and shopped in Vence, was known for his paper cutouts, and the bread, more commonly known as fougasse, *or "crazy bread," is cut like paper before it is baked.*

MAKES 6 SMALL RUSTIC LOAVES
- 1 cup warm water
- 1 package active dry yeast
- 2 tablespoons sugar
- 5 cups flour, divided
- 1 cup warm milk
- 2 tablespoons kosher salt

⊙ Put the water in a large, warm mixing bowl. (If your house is cooler than 70°F, warm the bowl by filling it with hot tap water and allowing it to stand for a moment; pour out the water and proceed.) Sprinkle the yeast over the surface of the warm water, then stir gently with a wire whisk to dissolve.

⊙ When the yeast is dissolved, stir in the sugar and 1 cup of the flour. Cover with plastic wrap and set aside for 1 hour to produce a "sponge," the foundation of all French bread.

⊙ After the "sponge" has risen, stir in the warm milk, salt, and another cup of flour. Exchange the wire whisk for a wooden spoon and stir in 2 cups of the remaining flour, a little at a time, stirring very well after each addition. Transfer the mixture to a floured surface and knead in just enough of the remaining cup of flour to create a very smooth, soft dough. Return the dough to the bowl and allow it to rise again until it is doubled in size, about 1 hour.

⊙ Preheat the oven to 400°F. Line two baking sheets with baker's parchment, or butter them lightly and sprinkle them with flour. On a well-floured surface, divide dough into 6 pieces, then press or roll each piece into a rough 6-inch circle. With a sharp knife, cut five or six 3-inch slits in each circle of dough, and stretch the dough slightly to open the slits. Put the flat breads on the prepared baking sheets and bake for 15 minutes, or until golden brown.

THREE SHELLFISH *with* THREE CITRUS FRUITS

The combination of shellfish and citrus fruit is so compelling to me that I have tried dozens of pairings. At Canlis restaurant, I started serving a trio of shellfish with three different citrus fruits. Since the scallops need to marinate, prepare them first.

EACH RECIPE SERVES 2

Scallops with Lime

4 very large scallops, about 1/2 pound
1 lime
1 tablespoon sugar
1 teaspoon kosher salt
12 radicchio leaves

⊙ Rinse the scallops, pat them with paper towels to dry, then slice each scallop across the grain into thirds to make a total of 12 thin scallop "coins"; set aside.

⊙ Using a zester, carefully remove the colorful outer rind from the lime and put it in a small mixing bowl. (If no zester is available, remove the outer rind with a potato peeler and cut it with a paring knife into very thin strips.) Juice the lime and add the juice to the zest. Stir in the sugar and salt.

⊙ Add the sliced scallops to the lime juice mixture and toss to coat. Chill the scallops in the lime juice for at least 30 minutes and up to 1 hour. Serve the marinated scallops on radicchio leaves.

Oysters *with* Orange

I dozen small, live oysters
I large navel orange

⊙ Keep the oysters right side up in a baking dish, covered with a clean, wet kitchen towel or several layers of wet paper towels. The bowl shape should be down and the flat "lid" should be up.

⊙ With a zester, carefully remove the colorful outer rind from the orange. Place the citrus zest in a small mixing bowl and set aside. (If no zester is available, remove the outer rind with a potato peeler and cut it with a paring knife into very thin strips.)

⊙ With a sharp paring knife, cut the tops and bottoms from the orange, then cut away the white pith and discard. Holding the fruit over the bowl of zest, cut out the sections of pulp, leaving the membranes of each section behind.

⊙ Carefully shuck the oysters, one at a time: Place an oyster cupped side down on a stable work surface. Using a towel to protect your hand from the sharp edges of the shell, hold the oyster firmly in one hand while you insert an oyster knife with the other. Push the knife in a short way and slide it under the top shell to cut the abductor muscle that holds the shell shut. Remove the top shell, then slide the knife under the meat of the oyster to free it from the bottom shell.

⊙ Put a small amount of the orange pulp and zest on top of each oyster and serve.

Crab Legs *with* Grapefruit

Dungeness crab is sold either live or cooked. It is also sometimes possible to pro-cure the shelled "fry legs" from a crab, but these are very expensive. The most practical approach is to buy a cooked crab, use the leg meat for this prepara-tion, and use the rest of the meat for another purpose. The presentation is very similar to the Belgian Endive and Grapefruit Salad with Goat Cheese Frit-ters on page 9.

Legs from I large cooked and cooled
    Dungeness crab, about 1½ pounds
I head Belgian endive (12 leaves)
I Ruby Red grapefruit
Grapefruit Vinaigrette (recipe follows)
A few leaves of spinach, cut into a
    chiffonade (about 2 tablespoons), see page 84

⊙ Remove the meat from the crab legs and discard the shells. Trim the base from the Belgian endive and pull off the individual leaves. Keep the crab legs and the endive leaves cold until just before serving.

⊙ With a zester, remove the colorful outer rind from the grapefruit and reserve. (If no zester is available, remove the outer rind with a potato peeler and cut it with a paring knife into very thin strips.) With a sharp knife, cut the top and bottom from each grapefruit, then cut away the peel; remove any bits of white membrane left attached. Working over a mixing bowl to catch juice, remove each section by cutting along the membranes on either side; there should be at least 12 sections. Cut in toward the center and then out. (Sections may be prepared several hours in advance.) Reserve juice for the vinaigrette.

◉ Arrange the leaves of Belgian endive in a palm-leaf pattern on a serving plate. Place a section of grapefruit in each leaf, and place the spinach ribbons at the base of the leaves. Place a crab leg in the cradle of each leaf and drizzle vinaigrette over the legs. Serve at once.

Grapefruit Vinaigrette

MAKES ABOUT 1/3 CUP

$\frac{1}{3}$ cup fresh-squeezed grapefruit juice

2 teaspoons sugar

$\frac{1}{4}$ teaspoon kosher salt

$\frac{1}{8}$ teaspoon ground white pepper

$\frac{1}{4}$ cup olive oil

◉ In a small nonreactive (stainless steel or enamel) saucepan, combine the grapefruit juice, sugar, salt, and white pepper. Over high heat, boil the mixture until it is reduced to $\frac{1}{3}$ cup. Take the pan off the heat. Add the olive oil in a thin stream while whisking the dressing until it is smooth and emulsified. Serve at once, or cover and keep refrigerated until serving time.

PROVENÇAL CHICKEN *with* TOMATO *and* ORANGE

The great French chef Auguste Escoffier, whose boyhood home in Villeneuve-Loubet is a few kilometers south of Vence, is credited with popularizing canned tomatoes. Here, canned tomatoes evoke the flavor of his native Provence. Organic canned tomatoes such as those from Muir-Glenn provide the best flavor.

SERVES 4

1 chicken (3 to 4 pounds), cut into 8 pieces

2 teaspoons kosher salt, or to taste

1/2 teaspoon freshly ground black pepper, or to taste

1/4 cup olive oil

1 medium onion, thinly sliced

4 cloves garlic, sliced

2 bay leaves

Grated zest and juice from 2 medium
    oranges, about 8 ounces each

1 can (14 1/2 ounces) diced tomatoes with
    their juice, preferably organic

⊙ Rinse the chicken and pat it dry. Sprinkle it liberally with the salt and pepper.

⊙ Put the olive oil in a heavy skillet over medium-high heat. When the oil is hot, place the chicken pieces skin side down in a single layer in the skillet. Cook the chicken pieces until the skin is golden, about 5 minutes, then turn the pieces over and cook for 5 minutes more. If the chicken begins to darken too much or if the oil begins to smoke, reduce the heat.

⊙ Remove the chicken pieces from the skillet, put them on a plate, and set aside. Pour off about half of the oil in the skillet (it will be a combination of olive oil and chicken fat). Sauté the onion in the oil left behind until it is soft and just beginning to brown, about 5 minutes. Add the garlic and bay leaves and sauté for 1 minute longer.

⊙ Put the orange zest, orange juice, and diced tomatoes in the skillet. When the sauce is boiling, put the chicken pieces back in the pan. Cover the skillet, reduce heat to medium low, and simmer until the chicken is tender and an instant-read thermometer registers 160°F when inserted into the thickest part of a drumstick, about 25 minutes.

⊙ Keep the chicken warm on a serving platter, and turn the heat up to high to finish the sauce. Simply boil it over high heat until it is reduced to a consistency you like. Depending on how much water evaporated while the chicken was cooking, this will take 2 to 10 minutes. Serve the chicken hot with the sautéed kale.

SAUTÉED KALE *with* GARLIC

Softened in olive oil, this green Mediterranean vegetable is a favorite at my house. Sliced thinly, the stems will cook as quickly as the leaves.

SERVES 2 TO 3

1 bunch curly green kale

2 tablespoons olive oil

4 cloves garlic, sliced

$\frac{1}{2}$ teaspoon kosher salt

$\frac{1}{4}$ teaspoon freshly ground black pepper

⊙ Rinse the kale and shake off the excess water. Stack the leaves with all the stems pointed in the same direction, and roll them lengthwise into a tight bundle. With a sharp knife, trim the stems and cut the bundle crosswise into $\frac{1}{4}$-inch ribbons. Greens may be cut in advance and refrigerated until just before serving time.

⊙ When you are almost ready to serve the greens, put the olive oil in a large saucepan over high heat. Add the garlic, salt, and pepper and then the greens. Cook for 1 or 2 minutes, moving the greens quickly around the pan with tongs until they are wilted. Remove from heat and serve at once.

CHOCOLATE MARQUIS *with* SAFFRON CREAM

Denser than chocolate mousse, almost like a chocolate truffle, this dessert may be served with the Saffron Cream presented here or with a simple fruit purée like the Strawberry Purée on page 21.

SERVES 4

> 6 ounces bittersweet chocolate
>
> 6 tablespoons (³/₄ stick) unsalted butter
>
> 2 medium eggs, separated
>
> ¹/₄ teaspoon salt
>
> ¹/₄ teaspoon vinegar
>
> 4 tablespoons sugar, divided
>
> 1 tablespoon dark rum
>
> 3 tablespoons heavy cream
>
> Saffron Cream (recipe follows)
>
> Chocolate Fans (recipe follows), optional

⊙ Line four 4-ounce ramekins with plastic wrap and set aside.

⊙ Put the chocolate and butter in a small saucepan over medium heat and stir until the chocolate is almost melted. Remove the pan from the heat and continue stirring until the chocolate is completely melted. Set aside.

⊙ In the bowl of an electric mixer or in a medium mixing bowl with a whisk, whip the egg whites with the salt and vinegar until they hold soft peaks. Stream in 2 tablespoons of the sugar and continue whipping until whites are stiff. Set aside.

⊙ Put the egg yolks in a small mixing bowl with the remaining sugar, and the rum. Whisk until the mixture is smooth, then whisk in the cream.

⊙ Stream the chocolate mixture into the egg yolk mixture, whisking all the while until the mixture is perfectly smooth; then gently fold in the egg white mixture. Promptly transfer the dense mousse to the prepared ramekins and chill for at least 1 hour.

⊙ To serve, invert the ramekins onto serving plates and peel away the plastic wrap. Drizzle the saffron cream around the chocolate.

Saffron Cream

Saffron, traditionally the world's most expensive spice (recent vanilla prices have soared into this realm and challenged this tradition), has a certain romance that is associated with both its rarity and its perfume. The intensely flavored red-yellow threads are the dried stamens of a fall-blooming crocus native to the shores of the Mediterranean Sea.

MAKES ABOUT ¹/₂ CUP
> ¹/₃ cup heavy cream
> 1 pinch saffron threads
> 1 egg yolk
> 2 tablespoons sugar

⊙ Warm the cream and saffron in a heavy saucepan over medium heat until it is steaming but not quite boiling.

⊙ Meanwhile, whisk together the egg yolk and sugar in a small mixing bowl. Stream the hot cream into the egg mixture, then transfer the sauce back to the pan and cook, stirring gently with a heatproof silicone spatula, until it is slightly thickened and steaming hot, about 5 minutes. The sauce may be served warm or cold.

Chocolate Fans

Easier than they look, vertical chocolate decorations are the finishing touch on professional-looking chocolate desserts.

MAKES 12 CHOCOLATE DECORATIONS
4 ounces bittersweet chocolate

⊙ Line a baking sheet with baker's parchment and set it aside. Chop the chocolate into ½-inch bits and put it in the top of a double boiler over barely simmering water. When the chocolate is about halfway melted, remove it from the heat and stir it until it is completely melted and smooth.

⊙ Transfer the melted chocolate to a self-sealing plastic food-storage bag and snip off a corner to create an impromptu pastry bag. Squeeze the chocolate onto the parchment-lined baking sheet in fanciful patterns and chill until the chocolate is firm. Peel the chocolate fans off the paper and plant them upright in any chocolate dessert.

From *the* Grill
A Steak Night

COCKTAILS

PARMESAN CHEESE CRISPS *and* SUN-DRIED TOMATOES
   with BASIL

CANLIS SALAD

GRILLED STEAKS *with* STEAK BUTTER *and* FRIED PARSLEY

NEW-TAKE TWICE-BAKED POTATOES

CHOCOLATE LAVA CAKES

I can see them even now: my mother with her hair done up in a sweep and her earrings catching the candlelight; my father stirring a pitcher of martinis and laughing, almost spilling the booze, at someone's off-color joke; and their friends, eating, talking, and singing songs at one of their famous dinner parties. Oh, they knew how to live!

When my parents got ready to throw a dinner party they cleaned house for days, arguing over piles of magazines and neglected heaps of stuff that had to be sorted through. They made us clean our rooms, sweeping aside our protests that their guests would never go in there. Then we had to rake the yard, sweep the driveway, and clean the windows. Sometimes they'd have the piano tuned or the carpets cleaned—

whatever it took to make the house shipshape. My father was, after all, a naval officer.

The refrigerator was cleaned out and restocked with food for the party. China plates were counted and silverware was polished. They bought tons of candles and filled all the hurricane lamps with oil. (For some reason they used only kerosene and candles to light the house on party nights—no glaring electric lights.) Bags of ice were hauled in. It was as if they were shoring up to face a natural disaster. Then they made a trip to the liquor store to stock the bar.

On the night of the party, the kitchen was filled with good smells—one of my mother's curries maybe, or shrimp Creole, simmering on the stove. The house was filled with flickering lights from the candles and the kerosene lamps, and the guests began to arrive. We were bustled upstairs and kept out of sight until we snuck back out to spy from the landing of the stairs, or to sneak drinks and hors d'oeuvres. Even though we weren't invited, all of us kids thought party nights were fun.

Those parties were in the 1960s and '70s, and the ebb and flow of getting the house ready for a dinner party two or three times a year, and then pulling it together after the storm had passed, seemed as normal as the changing of the seasons. I thought everyone did that kind of thing. And naturally, I assumed that when I was grown up and had a home of my own, I would throw parties just like those. But now here I am, ostensibly all grown up, and I have to say, I've never had a party like that.

Maybe those parties were a product of the era, or maybe my parents and their friends were bolder or more prosperous than we are. Maybe it's because I'm a chef, so hosting a dinner party would be a kind of busman's holiday. (And because I'm a chef, I don't get a lot of dinner invitations; people are afraid to cook for me.) For whatever reason, dinner parties at my house tend to be tamer than my parents' parties were, and they usually seem to commemorate something, like a birthday or Christmas. Or else they have a purpose—like entertaining coworkers. Our parties tend to be more spontaneous and less formal than my parents' were. We cook more and clean less, eat more and drink less.

Sometimes, though, when we have invited friends or even members of our own extended family over for dinner, the spirit of my parents seems to possess me. I clean out the fridge. We make the boys clean their room. We buy fancy beeswax candles for the dining room. And we obsess about the menu. This is the stage at which my feet begin to grow a little cold. It occurs to me that I have actually invited real living people into our humble family home.

I desperately wrack my brains for a solution. Our house's best feature is the garden, so we'll feed them out there. But even the garden is usually a mess, with weeds invading every bed and a rambling grapevine taking over the far side. By the time I clean it up, there will be no time left to cook. Bottom line, how could we possibly expect real people to dine in the middle of this menagerie of kids, snakes, birds, dogs, and goldfish? Oh well, I always think in the end, what's the worst that can happen? They'll see what a mess we really are. I try to stop worrying and plan the menu.

My first inclination is to wax elaborate, then I gradually pare down the frills until I'm left with a straightforward series of dishes that follow some simple theme, or at least have a kind of natural affinity for one another. I like to serve courses. This ensures that if one thing is less than perfect, at least there will be an opportunity to make amends when we clear away the plates and bring out another dish. Actually, it serves to keep things fun.

Start with some simple passed hors d'oeuvres and a glass of something tasty. Sit down to a good soup or salad, then clear it away before

211

you present the main dish. I like to put the soup bowls or the salad plates on top of the dinner plates. If the main course is to be served on a platter, the soup or salad dishes are taken away, and the dinner plates are already in place. And if the main dish is to be served on individual plates, the dinner plate can be carried away with the soup or salad plate for a quick wipe with a paper towel before the entrée is plated in the kitchen. Inevitably, at least one guest will be more comfortable helping with the clearing and plating than they would be staying at the table.

The change in scenery on the tabletop offers a chance to redirect the conversation. (With family gatherings this is often a very welcome opportunity.) Bring out the main dish—it can be on individual plates or on a platter to be passed around family style—and linger over this course. Finally, clear away the main course and bring out the dessert. Like one of those eleven-o'clock torch songs in an old-fashioned Broadway musical, the appearance of dessert wakes everyone up, re-engages their senses, and gets them ready for the last scene, during which all conflict will be resolved, all unanswered questions will be satisfyingly addressed, and everyone who was lonely or confused will be happily befriended and at peace.

This menu, which hearkens back to that era when my parents had dinner parties for their friends, is based largely on the kind of food I served when I was the chef at that great beacon of twentieth-century glamour and nostalgic ambience known as Canlis restaurant. At a time when the Weber grill was a novelty for budding backyard grill masters, Canlis put a big grill at the center of a formal dining establishment and brilliantly captured the casual elegance of that era, preserving it for future generations. This menu is a toast to Canlis and, by the same token, it is a tribute to my parents, who celebrated many major family triumphs with a steak night.

The Day Before

I used to tell my cooking students, who were forever wanting to know if this or that thing could be made ahead, that the ideal menu would allow them to do so much ahead that on the day of the party, they would need only to set the table and take a bath. This menu does allow the host to get a lot of the work out of the way before the guests arrive. Cheese crisps and sun-dried tomato topping for the hors d'oeuvres can both be made a day ahead. The twice-baked potatoes can be baked once, hollowed out and filled, and then refrigerated. The individual chocolate cakes should be made in advance and chilled well before they are put in the oven during dinner.

What to Pour

With the salad, it would be all right to pour water and allow the guests to finish and recover from their cocktails. The steaks deserve a big red wine like a Washington syrah or Bordeaux-style blend. With dessert, consider offering port.

Make It Simpler

The cocktails described below are fun, but a choice of sparkling wine or sparkling water would be easier. Instead of Parmesan crisps, consider serving smoked almonds in one dish and flavorful olives in another.

On the Table

With its classic simplicity, this meal is flexible enough to go from country casual to city formal. Whether it's served by the fireside in winter or at a picnic table in the summer, it should be served by candle-light.

COCKTAILS

For very good reasons, entire books have been devoted to the art of the cocktail, and for equally good reasons, many people eschew these drinks altogether. But to my mind, a simple cocktail, like a good steak, has a place now and then in a healthy life, and it seems to me that a selectively stocked liquor cabinet evokes a sense of well-being. No more than one or two cocktails should be served. Any more would render dinner a moot point. What makes these cocktails classic is both their enduring popularity and their profound simplicity. Neither one has any busy mixers like juice or soda; they are simply spirits presented in a simple and elegant way to ease the transition from everyday life to the make-believe world of the dinner party.

The Martini

Essentially a glass of well-chilled gin graced with a whiff of dry vermouth and an olive, a perfect martini is so simple a concoction that it hardly merits a recipe. There is a great deal of debate, though, about how best to make this cocktail as dry as it should be. My solution is to wet the ice cubes with vermouth and then discard most of the vermouth, leaving behind only its scent, before adding the gin. A minimum of stirring prevents the ice from melting and diluting the gin.

SERVES 2
> Ice
> 1 ounce dry vermouth
> 4 ounces gin
> 2 large green olives, preferably stuffed with garlic